multinational product management

edited by: **warren j. keegan**
george washington university
and
charles s. mayer
york university

AMERICAN **MARKETING** ASSOCIATION

222 S. Riverside Plaza • Chicago, IL 60606 • (312) 648-0536

Soc
HF
5415.15
M84

Cover Design by Mary Jo Galluppi

Library of Congress Cataloging in Publication Data

Main entry under title:

Multinational product management.

    Proceedings of a workshop held in Cambridge, Mass., Jan. 18-20, 1976, cosponsored by the Marketing Science Institute and the American Marketing Association.
    1. Product management--Congresses. 2. Export marketing--Congresses. I. Keegan, Warren J. II. Mayer, Charles S. III. Marketing Science Institute. IV. American Marketing Association.
HF5415.15.M84   658.8'4   77-5569
ISBN 0-87757-092-2

TABLE OF CONTENTS

FOREWORD

This volume represents the proceedings of a Multinational Product Management Workshop which was held in Cambridge, Massachusetts, January 18-20, 1976, cosponsored by the Marketing Science Institute and the American Marketing Association.

Marketing in a multinational setting has become an area of increasing interest to marketing managers. Managers and researchers alike in the United States and overseas have expressed a strong interest in improving the state of the art in this field.

The AMA/MSI Workshop was developed to provide an opportunity for a group of experts with a variety of interests and background experiences to exchange ideas and perspectives on issues and problems of multinational product management. The Workshop represented an open exchange both of research findings and of ideas.

Among the specific issues discussed were:

- Multinational product planning

- Screening criteria for identifying international product markets

- Experience transfer in multinational marketing management

- Multinational marketing management control systems

- Marketing research and multinational marketing management

- Information needs and research priorities in multinational marketing management

To Warren Keegan and Charles Mayer should go the credit for the planning and substantive elements of the conference. Judy F. Kugel of MSI's research staff served in her usual capable fashion as the coordinator of workshop arrangements.

We hope that those who are involved in the conduct of international marketing, as well as those in the business and academic community who are interested in studying it, find this volume of interest.

(Professor) Stephen A. Greyser
Executive Director
Marketing Science Institute

PART ONE

MULTINATIONAL PRODUCT PLANNING

NEW MYTHS AND OLD REALITIES

by Warren J. Keegan *

Today, more than at any time since the end of World War II, the multinational product planner faces major uncertainties in the world business environment. In Peter Drucker's prophetic phrase, business-people today must plan and operate in an "age of discontinuity." Table 1 summarizes the major discontinuities that have become apparent.

This paper focuses on the broad implications of the present international situation from the perspective of the multinational product planner faced with the task of formulating an overall strategic design for a multinational product plan. One of the potential hazards that the multinational strategic planner must contend with is the ever-present danger of accepting superficial, popular versions of global reality. My intent here is to focus on objective realities and, wherever possible, to identify myths that have been created by the fantasy of "current affairs." In addition, I propose a simplified method for grouping markets for planning purposes that helps identify where the greatest marketing opportunities are today.

THE INTERNATIONAL ECONOMY TODAY:
A REALISTIC PICTURE

Let us begin by examining the facts and realities of the international economic order. For the past two decades, manufacturing enterprises in the Western market economies have been steadily expanding their global reach. This expansion, while including the traditional exporting and importing of goods and services, has increasingly

---

*Warren J. Keegan is Professor of Business Administration at the School of Government and Business Administration, The George Washington University, Washington, D.C.

Table 1

THE POST WORLD WAR II WORLD ECONOMY—TWO PERIODS

Dimension	1946-71	1971-75
Economic growth	Steady growth	Stagnation
Price levels	Relatively stable, modest inflation	Double-digit inflation
Real income	Rising	Declining
Terms of trade	Declining for developing countries	Rising for developing countries
Global economic integration	Rising	No change or declining
Multinational corporations	Growing importance, support	Widespread criticism
Nationalism	Declining importance	Rising importance
U.S. imperialism	Rising	Declining
U.S. dollar	Growing importance	Declining importance
Technology	Profitable extensions and developments	Costly obstacles
Resources	Abundance	Scarcity
Psychology	Optimism	Pessimism

been based on investments in marketing, manufacturing, research and development, and engineering that are linked together in the framework of a global strategic plan. By 1971, the estimated production from foreign-controlled manufacturing investments in market economies was 106% of the exports of these countries. For mature international investor countries such as the U.S. and Switzerland, foreign production as a percent of exports was 396% and 236%, respectively.[1] Since World War II, world exports have been growing slightly faster than the gross world product, and international production has been growing faster than world exports.

In 1958, as Table 2 indicates, gross world product was $884 billion, world exports were $105 billion, and international production (production of foreign-controlled manufacturing investments) was roughly $90 billion. Total international business sales volume, the sum of world exports and international production, was $195 billion, or 22% of gross world product.

In 1973, gross world product was $4,400 billion, world exports were $550 billion, and international production was an estimated $550 billion. Total international business sales volume was $1,100 billion, or 25% of that year's gross world product.[2] During the past fifteen years, there has been a slight increase in the export intensity of the world economy and a 20% increase in the intensity of international production.

The old reality that underlies the world economy described in Table 2 is the concentration, particularly for manufactured products, of trade, investment, income, and markets in the industrial countries. In 1973, the most recent year for which global data are available, the United States, Western Europe, Eastern Europe, Japan, Oceania, and Canada accounted for 85% of the world's gross domestic product (GDP) and only 27% of the world's population (see Table 3).

The market characteristics of the industrial economies are determined not only by their aggregate size, but also by the fact that income per capita in these countries is relatively high, averaging well over $4,000. With the exception of products where government regulations and controls interfere with market allocations (e.g., television receivers, which are dependent on the availability of broadcasting which may be a government monopoly) or where other

5

Table 2

INTERNATIONAL BUSINESS
AS A PERCENT OF GROSS WORLD PRODUCT

Item	1958 U.S. $ Billions	1958 %	1973 U.S. $ Billions	1973 %
1. Gross world product	884		4,400	
2. World exports	105	11.8	550	12.5
3. Estimated international production[a]	90	10.2	550	12.5
4. Total international business sales volume (Col. 2 + Col. 3)	195		1,100	
International business as a percent of gross world product (Col. 4 ÷ Col. 1)		22.0[b]		25.0[b]

[a] Estimated value of all production owned by foreign investors.

[b] International business is a sales or turnover figure, while gross world product is a value-added figure that is net of purchases and resales. Thus, the two figures are not comparable; they do, nevertheless, give one measure of the intensity of international activity in the world economy.

Data sources: GATT, *Trade Network Table* and United Nations, *Statistical Yearbook,* various issues. Table prepared by author.

factors such as climate create a special situation (e.g., affect demand for air conditioners or heaters), gross national product per capita explains 70% or more of consumer product demand variance.[3]

In applying this rule to a developing country, it is important to carefully examine income distribution in the particular country. A low average per capita income may conceal a significant regional segment with a high average income that shares the market characteristics of countries with similar income averages. Sao Paulo, Brazil, for example, is more a European-type market for consumer products than a typical "average" Brazilian market.

Table 3

GLOBAL INCOME AND POPULATION
1973

Country or Area	GDP $ Billion	Population (Millions)	GDP/Capita $	% World GDP	% Population
United States	1,282	210	6,105	27	6
Western Europe	1,297	253	5,126	27	7
Eastern Europe	875	355	2,465	18	10
Japan	415	108	3,843	9	3
Oceania and Canada	186	38	4,895	4	1
Latin America (LAFTA, CACM, and Caribbean)	210	302	695	4	8
Asia (excluding Japan)	322	1,938	166	7	53
Middle East	69	104	663	1	3
Africa	94	331	284	2	9
Global total	4,750	3,639		99	100
Global average			1,305		

Data source: Business International, "Indicators of Market Size for 131 Countries," 1975 reprint edition. Table prepared by author. New York, Business International.

Demand for industrial products *in general* is closely related to gross domestic product per capita, which is the best single indicator of the degree of industrialization of an economy. Again, however, special circumstances must be taken into account. For example, certain oil-producing countries have very high gross domestic product per capita incomes that are based on sales of crude petroleum rather than on an industrial base. Demand in these countries is related to the priorities of the national government, which may be heavily focused on particular sectors, such as national defense. In other cases, historical specialization and success create focused industrial product demand. For example, the mining equipment industry in Sweden, the automobile industry in Germany, the camera industry in Japan, and the aircraft industry in the U.S. are particularly strong economic sectors and present focused industrial product needs.

World exports are similarly concentrated in the industrial countries, as can be seen in Table 4. In 1974, the industrial countries accounted for 64% of the world exports of all goods and 83% of the exports of manufactures.

Not surprisingly, foreign direct investment is also concentrated in the developed countries. Since it is difficult to obtain current data on world foreign direct investment, I examined instead U.S. foreign direct investment.[4] In 1974, as shown in Table 5, 82% of U.S. foreign direct manufacturing investment was placed in the developed countries. Indeed, if Brazil and Mexico, which account for almost two thirds of U.S. manufacturing investment in Latin America, are added to the developed countries, together they account for 91% of U.S. foreign direct manufacturing investment in 1974.

The economic reality of the world today is the domination by the industrial countries of Europe, North America, and Japan. The major factors in the development of this reality in this century are:

1. The greater internationalization of the world economy, particularly since 1945, as reflected by the growth of world trade and investment.
2. The gradual erosion of the dominant position of the U.S. since 1945 when, victorious and untouched, it accounted for more than half of gross world product as compared to the

8

Table 4

WORLD TRADE PATTERNS, 1971 AND 1974

	1974		1971	
Type of Exports	U.S. $ Millions	%	U.S. $ Millions	%
(A) Exports to the World— All Goods				
Industrial Areas*	544	64.2	251	71.5
Eastern Trading Area	71	8.4	63	18.0
Developing Areas	233	27.4	36	10.5
World Total	848	100.0	350	100.0
(B) Exports to the World— Manufacturers				
Industrial Areas*	398	83	187	84
Eastern Trading Area	43	9	23	10
Developing Area	38	8	14	6
World Total	479	100	224	100
(C) Exports to the World— Primary Products				
Industrial Areas*	119	36	51	46
Eastern Trading Area	24	7	12	11
Developing Areas	192	57	47	43
World Total	335	100	110	100

*Includes Australia, New Zealand and South Africa.

Tables prepared by the author.

Data sources: GATT, *International Trade,* 1974-75, Geneva, 1975, Table F
for (A) and Table E for (B) and (C).

Table 5

U.S. FOREIGN DIRECT MANUFACTURING
INVESTMENT POSITION—1974

Countries	U.S. $ Millions	%
Developed countries		82
Canada	$ 13,446	
Europe	23,765	
Japan	1,533	
Australia, New Zealand, and South Africa	3,048	
Total, developed countries	41,792	
Developing countries		18
Latin America	7,487	
Other Africa	160	
Middle East	130	
Other Asia and Pacific	1,344	
Total, developing countries	9,121	
All countries	$ 50,913	

Data source: U.S. Department of Commerce, *Survey of Current Business* (Washington: U.S. Government Printing Office, October 1975), p. 53, Table 13. Table prepared by the author.

present 27% share. This decline reflects the success other countries have had in "catching up" with the U.S.
3. The rise of Japan—and the decline of Britain—as a world economic power.
4. The establishment of a working international financial system which has resulted in widespread convertibility of currencies, particularly among developed Western or market economies.

5. The shift, since 1973, in world income from the industrial to the oil-producing countries.

MYTHS IN INDUSTRIAL ECONOMICS

Confronting these realities are a number of important, and potentially misleading, myths.

The first major myth that the multinational product planner must evaluate is the purported importance of less-developed countries (LDCs). The widespread attention given to the problems and needs of these countries in the United Nations and other international forums should not distort the fact that in 1973, as shown in Table 3, they accounted for only 14% of the world's gross domestic product. The fact that these countries accounted for almost three quarters of the world population in that year may turn out to have important longer-range geopolitical significance, but for the present, less-developed countries represent only 14% of the world's total purchasing power. Japan, for example, with only 5% of Asia's population, accounted for 56% of that region's gross domestic product in 1973. While none would rank Japan as equal to China as a geopolitical-military force in world affairs, it is an inescapable fact that currently Japan is a concentrated market of far greater importance than all the rest of Asia combined. India's total gross domestic product in 1973 of $60 billion was only one seventh of Japan's. China, with 22% of the world's 1973 population, had a total gross domestic product in 1973 only slightly larger than California's.

The simple fact is that most underdeveloped countries are neither important markets nor interesting locations for investment by multinational manufacturers. This is not true, of course, for the resource-extracting enterprises in industries such as petroleum and copper, although they have faced and will continue to face nationalization and expropriation of their "property" in less-developed countries. But their experience should not be allowed to cloud the picture for the manufacturing companies.

Economists and philosophers are properly concerned about the place and prospect of LDCs in the world economy. This attention should not confuse the marketing planner in a manufacturing

11

company. Market potential exists principally in those countries with high per capita incomes. The poor countries of the world, with low per capita incomes, are only limited markets for manufactured goods. Indeed, their potential importance for manufactured goods is less than their 14% share of gross world product, because a relatively higher percentage of the GNP in less-developed countries is required for food, clothing, and shelter than in the industrial countries.[5]

The second myth of multinational markets is the importance of opportunity in Eastern Europe, in particular the Soviet Union. There is no question that Eastern Europe represents a major share of gross world product (18% in 1973). The reality, however, is that the degree of integration between the Eastern planned economies and the Western market economies is far less than would be expected on the basis of the share of gross world product of these countries. In 1973, for example, world exports to the Eastern trading area accounted for only 4% of total world exports. The absence of a market allocation system in the Eastern economies presents a major barrier to trade and investment. The apparent source of this barrier is the shortage of foreign exchange available to the Eastern countries and the incompatibility of private ownership and equity foreign investment with the Marxist philosophy of state ownership of the means of production. More fundamentally, the real problem is the limited ability of Eastern enterprises to compete in Western markets. This restricts their opportunity to earn foreign exchange and thus to buy Western goods and to cover remittances of royalty, license, capital, and dividend payments of investors.

There is some evidence, particularly in the smaller border states of Eastern Europe, of a shift in resource allocation and management to the enterprise level. This move toward decentralization is accompanied, at least in dealings with the West, by an interest in adopting a market-oriented approach to management. If this tendency continues to grow, the ability of the Eastern countries to earn foreign exchange will be enhanced, and the importance of these countries as markets will expand commensurately. This, however, is a future possibility, or even likelihood, rather than a current reality.

The third myth of multinational markets is the inflated size of the import markets in the OPEC countries. There has been an important shift in real income to these countries since 1973, but this should be considered in the perspective of total world trade. OPEC revenues in 1974 were $105 billion, or 12% of that year's total trade of $848 billion. Their imports in 1974 were $50 billion and in 1975, $80 billion. These are sizable sums that represent the fastest growing new market area in the world today. Nevertheless, although the size of these markets is important, they are far from dominating the total trade network.

GROUPING WORLD MARKETS FOR PRODUCT PLANNING

The large number of countries in the world (at present count, more than 140) demands some simplified grouping of markets for planning purposes. A number of efforts to group world markets have been undertaken, most recently using factor and cluster analysis.[6] These efforts have been useful, but they are limited by their reliance on historical data that do not reflect the concerns of the practicing product planner about the future. To fill this gap, I have developed a typology based on five criteria: market size, market accessibility, stage of market development, present and future prospects for growth, and political risk. The use of these criteria has resulted in the four-category typology shown in Table 6.

The application of this typology requires analysis of the individual countries to categorize them according to their market accessibility and expected rate of future growth. Market accessibility will vary from company to company because of product differences, and expected future growth must necessarily reflect judgmental evaluation of country prospects. It is beyond the scope of this paper to engage in this kind of detailed analysis. However, to give the reader an idea of the order of magnitude of the various categories in the typology, I have, using the 1975 *World Bank Atlas* for 1973, assigned the 125 countries of the world with populations of more than one million to the typology categories using the following arbitrary criteria:

1. *Industrial countries:* All countries except OPEC members with a GNP per capita of more than $1,000. Eastern Bloc planned economies in this range are shown separately.
2. *Industrializing countries:* All countries with a GNP per capita between $500 and $1,000, plus OPEC members with higher and lower GNPs per capita.

Table 6

WORLD MARKETS FOR PRODUCT PLANNING—1973
COUNTRIES WITH POPULATIONS OF ONE MILLION OR MORE
1973 GNP (U.S. $ thousands)

Typology Category	Large-Scale Economies GNP: > $100 Billion		Medium-Scale Economies GNP: $25-100 Billion		Small-Scale Economies GNP: < $25 Billion		Total		
	GNP	No.	GNP	No.	GNP	No.	GNP	No.	%
1. *Industrial countries*									
a. Western market economies	$2,690,220	7	$424,250	10	$ 109,450	11	$3,223,920	28	57
b. Eastern Bloc planned economies	506,490	1	162,530	3	54,190	3	723,210	7	13
2. *Industrializing countries*									
a. OPEC countries	—	0	27,830	1	47,310	4	75,140	5	1
b. Other industrializing countries	—	0	126,780	2	83,430	15	210,210	17	4
3. *Promising less-developed countries*	216,750	1	—	0	149,320	42	366,070	43	7
4. *Unpromising less-developed countries*	—	0	71,590	1	948,500	24	1,020,090	25	18
Total	$3,413,460	9	$812,980	17	$1,392,200	99	$5,618,640	125	100

Data source: *World Bank Atlas* (Washington, D.C., 1975). Table prepared by author.

14

3. Promising less-developed countries: All countries with GNP per capita between $130 and $500, excluding OPEC members.
4. Unpromising less-developed countries: All countries with a GNP per capita less than $130.

The results of this exercise are shown in Table 6.

The Best Bet: The Industrial Countries

As I have already pointed out, the greatest opportunity in the world today lies in the industrial countries, particularly in the Western market economies. These countries not only represent the biggest markets, but they are also the most stable politically. Their political stability is assured by two forces. The first is the tendency of prosperous countries to prefer centrist government and rule of law as a strategy for keeping and building on what they have. Even in countries like France, which has a propensity to indulge in left-of-center political rhetoric, there is a realization that centrist policies have resulted in economic success and prosperity. This same rule explains at least part of the underlying support of successful nondemocratic governments in countries like the U.S.S.R. A second force that limits the tendency of these countries to apply discriminatory policies to "foreign" enterprise is the fact that most of these countries are the home base for companies who have invested abroad and who in effect have created national hostages in the form of their own foreign investment position. Where this is not the case, as in Canada, there is an absence of countervailing pressure to limit nationalist policies and restrictions and a tendency for nationalist and discriminatory government actions directed toward "foreign" enterprise.

As the process of economic convergence between the East and West continues, I expect an accompanying expansion of trade and investment or investment-equivalent opportunities in the East. As Eastern economies continue to decentralize, it is likely that they will become increasingly successful in competing in Western markets; this will enable them to expand their Western purchases. At some point, Eastern companies will no doubt wish to strengthen their position in Western markets through investments in marketing and, eventually,

15

even in manufacturing. When this interest develops, and is expressed, presently unimagined solutions to the obstacles to equity investment in Eastern countries will no doubt emerge. To be sure, this equity investment will probably not be called by that name, but the control and claim on income associated with equity investment could be obtained without the legal form of equity, thereby overcoming ideological objections to private ownership.

Important Potential: The Industrializing Countries

The rapidly industrializing countries, those whose real growth exceeds 5% per annum, present interesting risk-reward trade-offs. The present market size of countries with major potential, such as Brazil, is actually no larger than the increase in GNP in a single good year in the United States. The economic importance of countries like Brazil lies more in their potential than in their present size. If they successfully transform their economies and in effect thrust themselves into the industrial country class, they will then acquire both the market size and the political stability associated with industrial countries. If they do not succeed, they will probably become politically risky and economically troublesome areas à la Argentina.

Some Prospects: The Promising Less-Developed Countries

These countries represent small markets with prospects for future growth. Because they have not yet demonstrated their ability to achieve sustained real growth in excess of 5% per annum, they have attracted fewer foreign investors and spawned fewer local entrepreneurs; therefore, their markets are typically less competitive than the rapidly industrializing countries. They are off the beaten track, and frequently they present opportunities to form a local monopoly to companies willing to invest in their future. They present an opportunity to move one step further in the risk-reward trade-off. The payoff in these countries will materialize if they successfully achieve the status of a rapidly industrializing country and then eventually enter the industrial category. The risk is that they will fail or falter in their industrialization process and will react to their problems in ways that damage the quality of their business environment.

16

Few Prospects: The Unpromising Less-Developed Countries

This category contains those countries whose problems, either natural or man-made, seem to preclude any medium-term prospect for successful industrialization. These countries, by definition, are uninteresting investment opportunities. They need help, but the kind of help they need cannot realistically be provided by private investors responsible to shareholders for return on investment. They have small local markets with no prospect for significant growth, and their political stability is constantly threatened by their lack of economic success.

SOME FINAL THOUGHTS

In sum, the old reality that underlies the international economy is the concentration of wealth in a handful of industrialized countries. This concentration has shifted in this century with the rise of Japan as a major industrial power and the precipitous decline of Britain. Europe and North America have retained their economic ascendancy, with the United States and Germany occupying the premier positions they have held throughout this century. In addition, Eastern Europe has been on the rise since the end of World War II, but the major barriers between the planned Eastern economies and the market economies of the West continue to limit trade and investment across the East-West boundary. A further, and very recent, development in the world economy is the major shift in world income to the oil-producing countries.

This continued concentration has been accompanied by a significantly greater degree of internationalization of the world economy as measured by the percentage of gross world product accounted for by trade and international production. International production in particular is concentrated in the industrial countries of Europe, North America, and Japan.

The importance of developing countries to multinational manufacturing companies is largely a myth. As has been the case throughout human history, the poor of the world outnumber the rich. Indeed, the comment in the New Testament "for ye have the poor always with you"[7] has never been more relevant than it is today.

17

From the perspective of the product planner seeking sales and earnings, the poor countries are a limited prospect. However, discriminating analysis, using the typology of world markets suggested in Table 6, can guide the product planner to those rapidly industrializing and promising less-developed countries that offer interesting risk-reward trade-offs, with the possibility of either a monopolistic situation or the rewards accruing to an early entrant who can establish a leading position. The alternative, expanding in industrialized country markets, inevitably involves competing against a group of entrenched, established local and international companies (unless a company possesses a unique product or technology). The choice depends on a company's capabilities, resources, and assessment of opportunity and threat in the alternative market situations. In deciding on the best strategy, there is no simple calculus that can provide an easy answer. As always, difficult decisions require the application of analysis and judgment, and the willingness to accept risk and assert sustained effort. It is hoped that this discussion has helped clarify the nature of the alternatives available and the risk-reward trade-offs associated with these alternatives.

REFERENCES

1.   United Nations, *Multinational Corporations in World Development,* ST/ECA/190 (New York, 1973), p. 159, Table 19.

2.   Data Sources: United Nations, *Statistical Yearbook,* various issues; International Monetary Fund, *International Financial Statistics,* various issues; GATT, *Network of Total International Trade Table,* various issues; United Nations, *Multinational Corporations,* ST/ECA/190.

3.   See, for example, Reed Moyer, "International Market Analysis," *Journal of Marketing Research,* Vol. 6 (November 1969).

4.   In 1971, the United States accounted for 52% of the stock of foreign direct investment of the market economies of the world. See United Nations, *Multinational Corporations,* ST/ECA/190.

5.   Of course, for companies whose inexpensive products are targeted on basic needs, the developing countries can be important

markets. For example, soft drinks, flavors, and fragrances are successfully marketed in developing countries.

6. See, for example, Eugene D. Jaffe, *Grouping: A Strategy for International Marketing* (New York: American Management, 1974); and S. Prakash Sethi, "Comparative Cluster Analysis for World Markets," *Journal of Marketing Research,* Vol. 8 (August 1971), pp. 348-354.

7. Matthew 26:11.

2

EVALUATING INTERNATIONAL PRODUCT LINE PERFORMANCE

*by Donald S. Henley **

It is generally accepted in international business that a corporation will obtain different rates of return from its various domestic and overseas business operations. There is nothing particularly startling in this observation, since conglomerate operations such as General Electric have for some years recognized the problems inherent in evaluating performance across a wide range of product-market-technology combinations. In the international arena, however, the willingness to accept differential returns between countries in any one specific product-market-technology combination has been largely based on the awareness of risks that are unique to international operations.

Two types of risk are confined largely to business activity that crosses borders: those associated with currency and those related to political intervention. In the former case, the issues are foreign exchange exposure (in either a translation or conversion sense) and currency convertibility. Regarding political intervention, the concern is generally expropriation and nationalization, although a variety of political actions affecting marketing, manufacturing, and financial variables can severely affect subsidiary profitability.

There has been a considerable body of literature devoted to political and foreign exchange risk. There has been very little analysis of marketing variables and their impact on subsidiary and product line profitability. Yet, the evidence suggests that the marketing area provides the greatest number of major blunders in international operations. This is not too surprising, given the behavioral nature of marketing.

---

*Donald S. Henley is Associate Professor of Marketing and International Business, Michigan State University, Lansing.

In this paper, we will develop an approach to comparative evaluation of product line performance. *Product line* refers to a group of related products that are taken to market through common distribution channels, advertising media, and sales agents. In this context, refrigerators, for example, would be considered a product line. A family of major appliances—for example, refrigerators, stoves, and dishwashers—is considered three product lines, not one. *Performance* is defined in terms of marketing return on investment (ROI). A number of company-specific and environment-specific variables are hypothesized to influence performance.

THE NEED FOR COMPARATIVE ANALYSIS

Comparative evaluation is concerned with the effect of environmental, as well as managerial, variables on operating results and performance. Unfortunately, much of the international marketing literature has been primarily descriptive of various marketing environments. Little progress has been made in relating environmental factors to differences in market behavior and management performance.[1] To some extent, the problem is conceptual, for there are any number of difficulties involved in defining and measuring environmental variables and then relating them to performance. Of great practical relevance is the problem of managing cross-country studies, which are costly and time consuming.

In marketing, one problem has been the tendency to look at multinational marketing from either a polycentric or ethnocentric approach: that is, from the perspective that markets are so dissimilar as to make any degree of standardization or centralized planning or control impossible, or that the cost advantages of standardization are so compelling as to make adaptation to local environments a nuisance.[2] Increasingly, however, competitive and market realities have forced change on multinationals of all countries. The great need is to recognize similarities and differences in various market areas, to develop coordinated strategic plans, and to manage and control the worldwide marketing effort.

Corporations can no longer afford the luxury of uncoordinated strategies and loose control. The days when American multinationals could enter foreign markets with substantial technological, managerial, and marketing skill advantages are past. Increasingly, foreign subsidiaries, as well as domestic divisions, are being faced with strong European and Japanese competition, not to mention the entrance of government multinational corporations (MNCs) from both the Third World and Eastern bloc countries. European and Japanese companies operating overseas are moving away from strategies based on exports from the home country and the placement of largely autonomous "tariff" subsidiaries, toward strategies that are integrative, coordinated, and multinational in scope.

Thus, the great challenge in the next decade will be the management of MNCs in an increasingly competitive and, perhaps, capital-short world. Recently firms in the U.S. have taken a hard look at the businesses they are in. A retrenchment to core operations is taking place. On the international scene this will manifest itself in a more searching look at the product-country-target market matrix. Management at the headquarters and regional levels will be under increasing pressure to rationalize and focus efforts on those activities that are most feasible in a global context.

A FRAMEWORK FOR ANALYSIS

The analysis of foreign operations has proved to be difficult, both conceptually and practically. Virtually all the literature in the area of performance evaluation focuses on financial variables. While at first blush the issues appear to be fairly straightforward, in fact they are quite complex. The equity position in any subsidiary is greatly affected by local attitudes, practices, and laws regarding debt-equity ratios, depreciation allowances, and dividend payments. Differential tax rates can greatly distort managerial performance if it is considered only on an after-tax basis. Furthermore, the effect of currency changes and translation methods on the various operating and balance sheet accounts complicates what at first glance appears to be a language- and culture-free measuring tool.[3]

With regard to marketing, there are a number of conventional variables that can be used to measure performance, such as market share, sales growth, gross and net marketing margin, and price realization. These all *appear* to be acceptable for international comparisons. However, differences in such factors as competitive practices, marketing institutions, and stage of the product life cycle in country markets will have their effect on profit.

To what extent do international marketing managers feel the need for greater precision in their international analyses? My limited research in the area suggests that there is a desire for more structure in evaluating sales and marketing strategy alternatives and results. Thus far, these managers have had to work largely on the basis of intuition and experience. While no one familiar with the complexities of business decision making doubts the importance of these elements, it is also true that an explicit framework of key variables and their likely interaction with marketplace performance would enhance decision making. The ongoing PIMS (Profit Impact of Marketing Strategies) study, sponsored by the Marketing Science Institute, provides a guide to the type of framework required in multinational marketing.[4]

As noted above, there are several variables that may serve as measures of marketing output or performance. Since, to most American firms, the ultimate performance measure is return on investments, we prefer to work with that measure as adapted to *marketing* performance. Thus, "return" should be measured in terms of net marketing margin: that is, sales less distribution, and marketing costs less manufacturing costs.

Defining *manufacturing cost* poses special problems in an international context. It is well known, for example, that transfer prices can be adjusted for a variety of corporate reasons to the detriment of any one particular subsidiary. Thus, some system of shadow pricing for internal evaluation purposes is needed. Such a system appears, however, to be more easily discussed than implemented.

Also, for a variety of corporate reasons, a country market may be serviced from an external manufacturing plant. Thus, in addition to transfer pricing difficulties, the manager is faced with insurance, freight, duty, and perhaps inventory costs that would be incurred with local manufacture. His product cost may well be higher than would be the case with local manufacture. (Furthermore, he may not be supplied with a product that has been appropriately adapted for the local market.) Again, if the purpose is to measure managerial performance, as well as the inherent profitability of country-product market, some cost accounting adjustment must be made.

24

With respect to "investment," the relevant measure is those liquid and fixed assets committed to marketing. Thus, we would include accounts receivable and finished goods inventory as the major assets supporting the marketing effort. In some cases, of course, the value of these assets is determined as much or more by manufacturing, finance, or general management as by marketing. Nonetheless, they can be appropriately viewed as a marketing or distribution investment. Fixed assets that relate to the marketing effort are generally found in either service facilities or distribution warehouses. Again, each company may well handle these activities elsewhere than in the marketing function, but we view them as assets necessary to take the product to market.

The main conceptual areas to be explored lie on the input side. What are the elements of the product-market environment that have a measurable impact on performance and that, taken reasonably into account, would permit us to evaluate management or the lack thereof and the "true" profit potential of a product in a given environment?

Five variables appear to have critical and direct bearing on the issue at hand. Briefly, these are: (1) market share, (2) degree of product-market match, (3) stage in product life cycle, (4) degree and type of competitive activity, and (5) nature of the marketing support system.

Market Share Implications

The importance of market share to product line profitability has been well defined and documented in recent years. Both the Boston Consulting Group's work and the PIMS studies have stressed the importance of market share.[5] The Boston Consulting Group, in particular, has placed great emphasis on market share as it relates to movement down the cost curve. And, as a corollary, considerable attention has been given to the management of the product-market share-growth matrix, that is, managing the product portfolio. General Electric has been an industry leader in product portfolio management, in which market share position is a key variable.

To what degree does market share impact relate to international performance? To answer this question, it may be necessary to look

25

at the relationships of market share to (a) manufacturing cost and (b) market position and strength. With regard to the former, it appears that the critical issue for a multinational firm may be whether it has sufficient *worldwide* market share to attain cost economies or has rationalized worldwide manufacturing more effectively than its competitors, or some combination of the two. Thus, for any individual country manager, profitability may be a function more of the *corporate* manufacturing position, if his market is supplied from external sources, than of his country market share. Conversely, managers operating in an environment where national policy has forced local manufacture—that is, tariff factories—may find that even high market share does not offset inherent diseconomies of scale. Thus, they may be doing very well relative to their country-market competitors, but not relative to their fellow corporate marketing managers who are operating in a more favorable manufacturing source environment. A priori, it is not clear what the effect of market share as it relates to manufacturing cost will be. A high degree of subtlety is required in the analysis.

The effect of market share on competitive position, on relations with channel members, and on consumer franchise is less ambiguous. Here, there is little question that market share substantially enhances market power. For example, a soft-drink bottler with a good market share in the U.S. was easily able to introduce additional flavors into the channel. However, in foreign markets where it lacked a strong consumer franchise and channel power, expansion of the line was more difficult, costly, and time consuming. For many industrial items, the market leader is more likely to get its price than are those producers whose competitive edge is price alone. The market leader not only has a strong product-service offering, but it also almost always has an information base that permits it to make more intelligent pricing decisions, especially on negotiated jobs. "Buy-in" business is rarely profitable. In sum, where market share is used widely, product line profitability is enhanced.

Degree of Product-Market Match

This variable refers to a critical issue in multinational product planning: the extent to which the product is extended, adjusted, or invented for a particular market area.[6] Few multinational marketing issues have proved to be so vexing. The rationale for extension (standardization) is, at first glance, quite clear: no product research or development is required, manufacturing technology and quality control procedures have been established, and promotional material can quite often be used after language translation. The benefits are fairly readily quantified. The costs, on the other hand, are not so easily identified and are less easily quantified. It is no easy task for a country manager to argue on the side of opportunity cost.

There is ample evidence, however, of the cost of a poor product-market match. General Electric's entrance into the German small-appliance market is a classic example.[7] Polaroid's introduction of the Swinger into France in the mid-to-late 1960s is another.[8] Indeed, it appears that marketing miscues of this nature are frequent. In some cases, the mismatch is less evident, but nonetheless is high in opportunity cost. For example, American automotive firms in Brazil for years offered a product that was large and expensive to an unreceptive populace. Volkswagen's Beetle, on the other hand, was an excellent product-market match and enjoyed a 70%-75% market share for a number of years.

Excessive concern with local market adaptation can be costly, too. In an increasingly multinational world, the manufacturing cost disadvantages of precisely matching a product to narrow country-market segments may be too severe. Phillips of Holland found that European product standardization in television was necessary to obtain R&D and manufacturing efficiencies, even at the expense of marketing revenue.[9] In the mid-1960s, Hoover U.K. wrestled with this same issue in an attempt to develop a washing machine that could be standardized for the European market.[10] In this case, the data pointed to a U.K. product and a continental product. Unfortunately, clear and unambiguous solutions are usually difficult to come by.

Organizational dynamics complicate the issue even further. A fairly large U.S. manufacturer of scientific instruments had set up a task force, composed of Americans and Europeans, to work on a major upgrading of one of its product lines. European sales were equally as important as American sales; however, the design work was to be done in America. Despite frequent meetings, the Europeans still felt that their input did not carry full weight, since the American marketing people were in continual contact with engineering. Thus, decisions were made de facto outside the task force. One of the major American automotive companies has had this same experience in trying to coordinate European and U.S. design.

Stage of Product Life Cycle

The product life cycle is one of the few integrative concepts in marketing. The changing marketing mix and profitability adjustments that occur over time have been thoroughly discussed in marketing textbooks and articles.[11] We need not review them here. However, it is useful to note that there are a number of unresolved issues in the literature regarding the shape of the curve, the impact of product class versus product form versus product type, and even the usefulness of the concept per se.

The concept has been empirically tested with nonconclusive results. Businesspeoples have found the concept difficult to use because of great uncertainty regarding the timing and duration of the various phases. In my opinion, many of the difficulties in application arise from the simplistic view that there is one cycle that can be applied to either product class, form, or type. The dynamics of competitive product policy require a far more sophisticated approach than is revealed in most of the literature on the subject.

Although the validity of the model may be questionable, it still must be considered a potentially powerful tool in international product planning and control. The use of product-extension strategies by many multinational firms suggests that country markets are in different phases of the cycle and that the astute firm can take advantage of this. It is extremely important to recognize, however, that product extension of a mature product in one market to the introductory phase in another market must be accompanied by appropriate marketing mix and strategy adjustments. The well-documented failure of Polaroid-Swinger in France, where a marketing mix and strategy that were working well in a mature market were transformed virtually whole to a market in early introduction, is indicative of the pitfalls.

If we are willing to live with, and adjust to, the problems that seem to be inherent in defining exactly where a product is in the life cycle, cross-country comparisons appear feasible. It is critical, however, to recognize also the different product class, form, and type aspects and to take them into account. To refer back to the Polaroid example, given a product class (instant development) in maturity in the U.S., a new product form (low-priced instant development) can be expected to move into growth fairly quickly. In France, however, the situation is one of new product class as well as of new product form. Thus, we expect a slower movement through introduction and, therefore, lower profitability than in the U.S.

Nature of Competition

We are well aware that competitive environments and attitudes toward competition vary widely around the world. This is partly a function of legal and philosophical differences. Yet it is equally a function of differences in the marketplace itself. Regardless of the underlying rationale, any cross-country comparison of product line profitability must take into account differences in competitive environment in the markets within which the firm operates.

Perhaps the most obvious differences can be found in the realm of legal and philosophical approaches to competition. Europe, Japan, and the U.S., for example, differ greatly in their public policy on competition. In the U.S., antitrust has a long history. Structure and conduct are the principal bases on which public policy toward competitive activity is formulated. In Europe, antitrust has a history of less than fifteen years. Performance is far more important than structure or conduct. The Europeans are prepared to permit structure and conduct that would be unheard of in the U.S., *provided* that performance is acceptable in terms of public benefits (price, products, service, stable employment, etc.). The Japanese, if the literature is to be believed, coordinate industry, financial institutions, unions, and governments in a manner impossible to duplicate in the other advanced countries. In the developing countries, antitrust is virtually unknown and competition may even be seen as wasteful of fixed plant and equipment.

There are also substantial differences in philosophy regarding competition. Americans extol the virtues of competition, although the extent to which there is price collusion suggests that competition is perhaps best left to the other person's industry. Europeans are less likely to view vigorous price and market share competition as a positive good. Until very recently, the tendency has been toward cartels and agreements. The Japanese are vigorous competitors in the other person's market, but they are not so sure they want strong competition in their own market, as witness Dow's attempts to develop a chlorine operation.

Of course, attitudes and practices are in constant flux, and it is dangerous to make generalized statements. The evidence is sufficiently strong, however, to warrant explicit consideration of the general legal and philosophical approaches to competition and their resultant effect on price and profits.

More specifically, we can consider the degree to which competition is tight or loose. Uyterhoeven and Hodgson explored various factors relative to the "tightness" of competition and to operating margins in a product-market setting.[12] While their work related to entry analysis and to Europe in the late 1950s and early 1960s, the concepts can be used for our purposes. In essence, they argue for explicit consideration of, among other things, the degree to which service is included in the product offering and the degree to which it is included in the price. In other words, operating margins may be high because service is not included or because the industry charges for it. In either case, the manager is the beneficiary. Or, service may be given away, with consequent impact on operating margins and profits.

Nature of the Marketing Support System

The final environment variable to be considered is the marketing support system. The *marketing support system* is defined as those institutions and functions that are necessary to create and service demand. Examples are media, retailers and wholesalers, sales representatives and agents, repair and service operations, warehousing and transportation, and credit. The external availability, performance, and cost of these various institutions can greatly affect the firm's marketing strategy and profitability. It is extremely important to take this factor into account when evaluating product-country profitability.

30

Most food distribution systems in Latin America, for example, provide virtually no merchandising support for processed food manufacturers.[13] The processor is, therefore, forced to internalize many of the demand-creating and servicing functions that are supplied by retailers, wholesalers, brokers, and the like, in the U.S. Consequently, costs are high and, depending on price flexibility, profits may be lower. For some industrial goods there are only a few quality distributors available, thus sales volume and hence profitability are affected if the firm cannot obtain the services of these distributors. Or, as was the case of Polaroid-France, the firm may be forced to expend a substantial amount of merchandising and promotion funds, as well as considerable sales manpower, to get the support of specialty shops. For Polaroid, on a per-unit basis this "push" strategy was more costly than the "pull" strategy used in the U.S.

Where external credit agencies are not normally available, and where credit can be an important competitive tool, management may choose to internalize this function. However, operating costs and marketing assets will both be higher than otherwise. Profits may or may not suffer.

A listing of all possible permutations of different marketing support systems is not necessary. Company management's job is to identify those elements that materially affect product line profitability and that are essentially outside the control of local managers.

SUMMARY

I have attempted in this paper to define the key *marketing* variables which appear to affect profitability in a variety of country settings. The purpose has been to make a beginning on an issue which will be increasingly important to businessmen in the decade of the 70's, the effective management of multi-country marketing operations in an increasingly competitive business world. More so than in domestic operations, management needs guidelines regarding the relative quality of performance in a variety of environmental settings.

It is clear that a full and complete framework has yet to be articulated. Some would argue that government regulations should be taken into account more explicitly. More precision is required

31

regarding the strength of causal relationships and the relative weightings of the variables. A great deal of empirical work remains to be done. Nevertheless, it is expected that this paper will move us further down the road toward more effective multi-country marketing management.

REFERENCES

1. For a pioneering effort in this area, See Robert D. Buzzell, "Can You Standardize Multinational Marketing?," *Harvard Business Review,* 45 (November-December, 1968), 102-113.

2. Research by Sorenson and Wiechmann suggest that there is a great deal of standardization by packaged consumer goods companies. However, their research was not able to provide hard data on the costs and benefits of such standardization. See Ralph Z. Sorenson and Ulrich Wiechmann, "How Multinationals View Marketing Standardization," *Harvard Business Review,* 53 (May-June, 1975), 38-54, 166-167.

3. For an early, but still useful, general review of financial issues in assessing multi-country performance, see Dan T. Smith, "Financial Variables in International Business," *Harvard Business Review,* 44 (January-February, 1966), 93-104.

4. See Robert D. Buzzell, Bradley T. Gale, and Ralph G. M. Sultan, "Market Share—A Key to Profitability," *Harvard Business Review,* 53 (January-February, 1975), 97-107.

   Also, Sidney Schoeffler, Robert D. Buzzell, and Donald F. Heany, "Impact of Strategic Planning on Profit Performance," *Harvard Business Review,* 52 (March-April, 1974), 137-145.

5. See Buzzell, Gale, and Sultan, *ibid.* Also, Patrick Conley, "Experience Curves As A Planning Tool," *IEEE Spectrum* (June 1970), 63-68.

6. For an excellent general framework, see Warren J. Keegan, "Multinational Product Planning: Strategic Alternatives," *Journal of Marketing,* 33 (January, 1969), 58-62.

7. See *Princess Housewares (A and B)*, ICH 13 M117/118, Intercollegiate Case Clearing House, Harvard Business School.

8. See *Polaroid—France (S.A.)*, ICH 13 M119, Intercollegiate Case Clearing House, Harvard Business School.

9. *Phillips Gloelampenfabricken (A, B and C)*, #9-374-032/33/34, Intercollegiate Case Clearing House, Harvard Business School.

10. *Hoover (A)*, #9-569-015, Intercollegiate Case Clearing House, Harvard Business School.

11. For example, Theodore Levitt, "Exploit the Product Life Cycle," *Harvard Business Review*, 43, (November-December, 1965), 81-94.

    Also, John Smallwood, "The Product Life Cycle: A Key to Strategic Marketing Planning." *M.S.U. Business Topics*, 21, (Winter, 1973), 29-36.

12. Raphael W. Hodgson and Hugo E. R. Uyterhoeven, "Analyzing Foreign Opportunities," *Harvard Business Review*, 40 (March-April, 1962), 60-79.

13. For a comprehensive review of food marketing systems in Latin America, see Kelly M. Harrison, Donald S. Henley, Harold M. Riley, and James Shaffer, *Improving Food Marketing Systems in Developing Countries: Experiences from Latin America*, Research Report No. 6, East Lansing, Michigan: Latin American Studies Center, Michigan State University, 1974.

3

AN INNOVATION-DIFFUSION PERSPECTIVE

by Georges P. LeRoy *

The rapid increase in the number of multinational firms, together with the greater complexity of their operations, suggests that these companies are able to prosper because they are devising original ways to tackle new challenges. One response to the increased complexity these firms are facing is to decentralize and let the various units define their optimal strategies. Alternatively, a company may respond by better *worldwide* corporate planning. Worldwide corporate planning means that the firm is looking at alternatives with a multi-country outlook, asking questions such as: Where in the world should we locate that plant? Where in the world should we market this product? Where in the world should we develop this product? Such planning of the production and marketing aspects may be performed before the initial launch of the product or, alternatively, only as the need arises. In this latter case, the product is generally developed in response to a particular country's opportunities. It may later be marketed abroad if favorable circumstances arise, success in the initial country being, as a rule, a prerequisite for introducing the product in other countries.

This paper outlines one important issue the multinational planner is confronted with: the determination of a preferred pattern of innovation and diffusion for his products. This issue is important because the speed at which a firm launches a product internationally can be critical to the financial success of the venture, particularly when competitors are in a position to react quickly. A problem of this nature arose recently with the Paris *haute couturiers,* who, faced with instant copying of their styles during their preseason fashion shows, innovated their own fabric designs and colors.

---

*Georges P. LeRoy is Associate Professor of Management, McGill University, Montreal, Quebec, Canada.

Similarly, the question arises with regard to the Renault 5: Was Renault right to wait three years to introduce the Renault 5 to the U.S., while the Honda Civic, among others, was being introduced practically simultaneously in both Japan and the U.S.?

Although the advantages of worldwide corporate planning at the product level (also called multinational product planning) vary from firm to firm, there still exist some very tangible benefits to be derived by any firm undertaking this type of planning. As part of an earlier work, I carried out a study of the innovation-diffusion patterns of products and gathered empirical evidence in five well-known multinational firms.[1] This paper is an outgrowth of that study, using data gathered for 52 products of those firms.

INNOVATION-DIFFUSION PATTERN RELATIONSHIPS

On the basis of these data, complemented by numerous interviews with managers of the firms, an analysis was made of patterns of innovation-diffusion and their relationships to various characteristics of the product, country, and firm. The innovation-diffusion pattern is described in terms of the particular path (alternatively called the multinational product strategy—MPS) followed and the speed of diffusion. Three main paths were identified: (1) export only (MPS 7), (2) export followed by production in the customer's country (MPS 1), and (3) production in the country without export (MPS 8).[2]

The speed of diffusion is expressed in terms of *market lags* and *production lags* between the country of initial marketing and the country in which the product is eventually introduced. The market lag for a given product introduced in country X is defined as the time lag between its initial introduction on the market and its introduction in country X. Similarly, production lag is defined as the time lag between the initial production in the country of origin and the start of production in country X.

The findings of the study, categorized by firms, are quite intriguing. For example, Table 1 shows that the average market lag for the electronics firm is one tenth that of the aluminum manufacturer and one sixth that of the toiletries manufacturer. One is tempted to

Table 1

MARKET LAGS AND PRODUCTION LAGS BY FIRM

Lag	Electronics Firms	Agricultural Machinery Firm	Aluminum Manufacturer	Visual Communication Equipment Manufacturer	Toiletries & Personal Care Manufacturer
Average market lag (in months)	4.7	21.7	55.8	5.0	30.1
Average production lag (in months)	36.0	64.0	62.0	6.0	50.0

Note: The average lag for the firm represents the lag between the country where the product was initially introduced and any other country over all the products selected in this firm and all the countries it was diffused to.
Source: Survey data.

explain these lags by suggesting that the electronics industry is a dynamic one with a high rate of innovation, but this is only part of the answer. Or one may question the representativeness of the 52 selected products. An in-depth study of those firms, however, found no systematic bias. Our intent here is to look at a number of characteristics that influence the innovation-diffusion pattern.

Product Characteristics

It was thought that the type of product, whether consumer or industrial, could account for some of the differences in behavior observed in the study. The product selection contained 12 consumer products which had an average market lag of 33.7 months; this contrasted sharply with the 10.1 months average lag for the 40 industrial products (see Table 2). This marked difference is to some extent due to the fact that consumer goods are in general more sensitive to cultural variables and usually require some modifications.

The consumer goods versus industrial goods categorization of products appears to affect not only the speed of diffusion, but also its pattern. One can see from Table 3 that consumer products have a greater likelihood of being introduced internationally by production close to the market (MPS 8). This suggests that product modifications are often best determined and implemented in close contact with customers.

One could also hypothesize that the choice of a pattern of diffusion is affected by the degree of novelty of the product. The firm will take a smaller risk of failure in international markets if it is already experienced with products that are not markedly different from the standpoint of performance. The figures in Table 4 are consistent with this hypothesis: the average market lag for totally new products is 18.4 months, while it is only 2.7 months for products that are minor modifications *in terms of performance* relative to the previous product the firm was marketing.

I explored the variation in market lags further. A similar question was asked regarding the technological novelty of the product, as this could have been a delaying factor from the manufacturer's point of view. Technological novelty refers to the newness of the production

Table 2

TYPE OF PRODUCT AS RELATED TO SPEED OF DIFFUSION (MARKET LAGS)

Type of Product/Firm	Total Market Lag for All Countries (in mos.)	No. of Observations	Average Market Lag
Consumer products			
Alcan (AL1, AL2, AL3, AL4, AL8)	590	10	59.0
Dymo (DY1, DY4)	60	8	7.5
Gillette (GL1, GL2, GL3)	362	12	30.2
Total	1,012	30	
Avg. market lag, consumer products			33.7
Industrial products			
Hewlett-Packard (HP1 to HP24)	367	78	4.7
Massey-Ferguson (MF1 to MF13)	826	38	21.7
Alcan (AL5, AL6)	24	1	24.0
Dymo (DY2, DY3)	39	7	5.6
Total	1,256	124	
Avg. market lag, industrial products			10.1

39

Table 3

TYPE OF PRODUCT AS RELATED TO PRODUCT STRATEGY IMPLEMENTED

| Product Strategy | Type of Product | | Proportion of Consumer Products (1)/[(1) + (2)] |
	Consumer (1)	Industrial (2)	
A. Diffusion from the U.S./Canada to Europe			
Strategy MPS 7 (export only)	0	17	0.0
Strategy MPS 1 (export & invest)	3	7	.3
Strategy MPS 8 (direct invest)	4	1	0.8
B. Diffusion from the U.S./Canada to Japan			
Strategy MPS 7 (export only)	2	16	.1
Strategy MPS 1 (export & invest)	2	7	.2
Strategy MPS 8 (direct invest)	1	0	1.0
C. Diffusion from any country to any other			
Strategy MPS 7 (export only)	5	65	.1
Strategy MPS 1 (export & invest)	7	14	.3
Strategy MPS 8 (direct invest)	8	2	.8

Note: Numbers in the body of the table correspond to the number of times a particular product strategy was observed.

Table 4

MARKET LAGS RELATED TO NOVELTY OF THE PRODUCT

	Degree of Novelty		
Area of Novelty	Totally New	Major Modifications	Minor Modifications
Novelty of performance			
Average market lag (in months)	18.4	16.8	2.7
Technological novelty			
Average market lag (in months)	12.0	13.4	25.0

process. Again looking at Table 4, we find that the degree of technological novelty does not appear to be an obstacle to rapid international diffusion of products. However, this result is influenced by
the fact that half of the observations classified as "totally new" in
technological novelty come from the electronics firm with the fastest
diffusion. There are a number of other product-related factors that
can alter the pattern, such as the ease of communicating the key
product features. The technological novelty of the product can also
have an effect on the pattern of innovation-diffusion selected by the
manager. We hypothesized that rather than delaying the entry of the
product in international markets until the market could support production, the manager might export before producing abroad, or
export instead of producing close to the market. Using data on diffusion from the U.S. or Canada to Europe (see Table 5), we can
observe that managers prefer to use a strategy of diffusion such as
export only (MPS 7) or export followed by production (MPS 1)
rather than direct production (MPS 8). Export is viewed as a way to
develop the market and reduce uncertainty.

Country Characteristics

The international strategy of the firm in terms of production and
marketing is also likely to be affected by the particularities of the
country. The level of income and buyer sophistication, or the patterns of consumption and the strength of demand, will influence the
firm's decision to penetrate a particular market.

In many instances, the decision maker has some freedom to
choose the most appropriate entry strategy. His range of choices is
best expressed in the adaptation-standardization dilemma.[3] From
the interviews with managers, it appeared that two factors were most
important in determining the degree of international standardization:
(1) the extent to which the firm was able to design a product that
was compatible with worldwide market needs, and (2) the kind of
competition the company faced in the various markets. To reach
international compatibility, these firms generally tend to upgrade the
product to meet the requirements of the country with the most
stringent product standards.

42

Table 5

NOVELTY OF PRODUCT AS RELATED TO PRODUCT STRATEGY IMPLEMENTED
(Diffusion from the U.S. or Canada, to Europe)

Area of Novelty	Degree of Novelty		
	Totally New	Major Modifications	Minor Modifications
Novelty of performance			
$R = \dfrac{MPS\ 8}{MPS\ 1 + MPS\ 7}$	1/9 $<$	1/3 $>$	0
Technological novelty			
$R = \dfrac{MPS\ 8}{MPS\ 1 + MPS\ 7}$	1/12 $<$	1/8 $<$	3/7

Note: Figures in the table correspond to the frequency of implementation of the product strategies.

43

Looking at international product diffusion (see Table 6), it may come as a surprise that market lags are generally quite short, the average being a little more than one year (14.6 months). An exception is noted for one product of the aluminum manufacturer Alcan, where the market lag between Canada and the United States is 60 months. However, one can see important differences between countries for the various firms. Hewlett-Packard, the electronics firm, has one of the smallest spreads of market lags between countries, ranging from 1.6 months to 7 months, while Massey-Ferguson's range is 24 months to 68 months.[4]

In a few cases, it was found that competition was keener in Europe; the product was not only developed to suit European standards, but it was also introduced in Europe first. In general, one would hypothesize that as the intensity of competition facing a product is stronger, the firm will act faster, thus resulting in smaller market lags. Table 7 presents the data for the 52 products using the managers' own appraisals of the general (worldwide) intensity of competition. Three firms—Hewlett-Packard, Massey-Ferguson, and Alcan—appear to agree fairly closely with the hypothesis. In view of the fact that few cases fell in the "low intensity of competition" category, our interpretation of the data has been confirmed by interviews.

For Hewlett-Packard, one would have expected a market lag greater than 3.3 whenever there is low competition. But, as we shall see in the next section, another factor overrides the competition effect.

Competition affects not only market lags, but also the particular path of diffusion selected. Our expectation is that the greater the competitive situation, the more likely the firm is to produce close to the market. From a marketing viewpoint—which includes feedback, visibility, and market aspects—this would appear to be a desirable state. The data in Table 8 confirm that the "export only" strategy is preferred when competition is low.[5]

In fact, the opinions that were expressed in the interviews were very much along the lines that extremely competitive activity in a market represents an opportunity for profits as opposed to a threat of losses. Whereas a classic analysis would suggest no commitment of

Table 6

MARKET LAGS BY FIRM AND BY COUNTRY
(in months)

Firm	Product First Marketed in Parent Country of Firm and Diffused to the Following Countries						Product First Marketed in a Host Country of Firm and Diffused to the Following Countries						Avg. Lag by Firm
	USA	Can.	Eur.	Japan	Latin Amer.	Avg.	USA	Can.	Eur.	Japan	Latin Amer.	Avg.	
Hewlett-Packard	–	3.5	6.1	7.0	1.6	4.9	2.0	3.9	0	3.5	4.2	3.3	4.7
Massey-Ferguson	0	–	24.0	42.0 (Australia)	68.0	47.2	11.5	5.0	0	11.8 (Australia)	28.6	14.1	21.7
Alcan	60.0	–	51.0	39.0	94.0	55.1	0	24.0	94.0	–	–	59.0	55.8
Dymo	–	0	5.0	8.0	6.0	4.6	5.0	5.0	0	8.0	6.0	6.0	5.0
Gillette	–	7.0	23.0	56.6	34.6	30.1							30.1
Average market lag (weighted)	60.0	4.1	14.5	17.2	19.7	15.8	8.3	6.0	94.0	9.0	20.6	12.2	14.6

Note: The lags are average lags for the firm or the country over the various products. Market lag is the time lag (in months) between the first introduction of the product in one country (X) and the introduction in another (Y). The "countries" at the top of the table are the Y countries, where the product was diffused to: "—" means not applicable, as by definition there is no lag for the country of initial introduction. The blank spaces for Gillette indicate that no corresponding observations were collected.

45

Table 7

MARKET LAGS RELATED TO INTENSITY OF COMPETITION

Intensity of Competition	Average Market Lags (in months)				
	H.P.	M.F.	Alcan	Dymo	Gill.
High	3.5	11.6[a]	33.8	9.0	40.0
Medium	10.5	20.1	36.0	6.0	10.0
Low	3.3	—	78.0	2.5	0

[a]Excludes one implement which had a very high lag.

investment resources in a competitive market before a market share has been achieved, the firms here tended to do just the opposite. They appear to meet the competition head on.

Firm Characteristics

After having analyzed the pattern of innovation-diffusion in terms of product and country characteristics, one could argue that firms have little freedom left. This does not appear to be the case, however, as the objectives of planning and organization may differ from firm to firm even within the same industry. As stressed by Robertson: "Marketing strategies can guide and control to a considerable extent the rate and extent of new product diffusion."[6]

Although at this exploratory stage no multidimensional analysis was performed with the data to try to separate the effects of the various product, firm, and country characteristics, they were visible as the interviews progressed.

If the speed of international diffusion is considered *one* index of efficiency, marked differences were clearly observed in this respect.

Table 8

COMPETITIVE SITUATION AS RELATED TO PRODUCT STRATEGY SELECTED

	Intensity of Competition		
Product Strategy	High	Medium	Low
Diffusion from the U.S./Canada to Europe			
Strategy MPS 7 (export only)	1	4	12
Strategy MPS 1 (export & invest)	5	1	4
Strategy MPS 8 (direct invest)	2	1	1
Frequency of MPS 7	1/8 = .12	4/6 = .66	12/17 = .70
Diffusion from the U.S./Canada to Japan			
Strategy MPS 7 (export only)	3	3	12
Strategy MPS 1 (export & invest)	3	1	5
Strategy MPS 8 (direct invest)	1	0	0
Frequency of MPS 7	3/7 = .23	3/4 = .75	12/17 = .70

Following is some evidence regarding planning and organization of the innovation-diffusion strategy using two very different types of management organization. This evidence indicates that management organized along product lines worldwide, rather than along geographic lines, has distinctly different effects on the product diffusion pattern and the length of the market lags.

Firm A develops and markets industrial products that are standardized worldwide. Until six years ago, product development and specifications were the responsibility of the parent company, who exported its products to foreign subsidiaries through its international division. The subsidiary abroad would ask for the transfer of production whenever this was economical from their point of view. Often the transfer had implications for the parent product division that resulted in delays and that appeared to the subsidiary as a lack of responsiveness by the parent. For example, the delays in the transfer of production were such that production lags of two years were very common. And often, rather than take into account worldwide product specifications, the parent subsidiary, being a profit center, would develop a product based on the specifications of its own market. In reaction to the problems caused, the company reorganized into worldwide product divisions, which resulted in the efficient coordination of domestic and international markets. This in turn led to increased sales, and production lags were reduced to three-to-six months.

Firm B is a manufacturer of industrial products that integrated forward a decade ago and now manufactures both consumer and industrial goods. While it used to have much of its primary technology centrally controlled in the parent country, it has now decentralized its production operations into independent geographic areas. Each country being a profit center, managers have to be persuaded that a particular technology is a good investment for them. Since transfers of products, or of technology, are not centrally located, worldwide product group coordinators must be used to help perform the communication and persuasion function.

As mentioned earlier, success of a product in one country is a necessary condition for its being adopted elsewhere. Products being generally developed for *one* particular market need to be adapted to suit other markets. This means longer diffusion lags and may also

48

lead to some duplication. Whether a firm can be satisfied by following a pattern similar to firm B will depend on the particular product it manufactures and how it may be affected by competitors' strategies, which may be more efficient.

These cases illustrate two quite opposite approaches to planning. For firm A, the concept of multinational product planning is a reality; the worldwide product manager considers alternatives on a worldwide basis. For firm B, the pattern of diffusion is a result of the decisions of a series of "independent" country managers. The linkages between subsidiaries are in one case an integral part of the structure, while in the other they are accomplished informally by committees.

CONCLUSION

Using a dynamic approach, an innovation-diffusion perspective, we have stressed that the pattern of innovation-diffusion is affected by a number of firm, country, and product characteristics.

Our research, albeit of an exploratory nature, suggests that the differences in the efficiency of innovation-diffusion can to some extent be controlled by the firm. A firm that adopts the worldwide product management approach appears to be better able to develop a product that has specifications compatible on a worldwide scale, and this results in smaller market lags. A firm that leaves product development up to independent units will incur greater difficulties in transfering its experience and technology, thus resulting in greater lags. Certainly, further study on a broader scale is warranted to confirm or dispel the conclusions we have reached.

REFERENCES

1. Georges P. LeRoy, *Multinational Product Strategies: A Typology for Analysis of Worldwide Product Innovation-Diffusion* (New York: Praeger, Special Studies in International Economics and Development, Spring 1976).

2. These three paths represent the most frequent alternatives used by these multinational firms to innovate and diffuse their products internationally. The full variety of paths is presented in LeRoy, *Multinational Product Strategies.*

3. Robert D. Buzzell, "Can You Standardize Multinational Marketing?" Vol. 46, *Harvard Business Review* (November-December 1968).

4. The reader may wonder why Hewlett-Packard is introducing its products faster in the Latin American market (market lag = 1.6 months) than in Europe (market lag = 6.1 months). The reason is that a number of products were not introduced into Latin America, therefore the market lag is infinite. However, infinite lags were not counted. This explains the apparent discrepancy.

5. For a detailed analysis of the factors that influence the production location see LeRoy, *Multinational Product Strategies.*

6. Thomas S. Robertson, "The New Product Diffusion Process," in *American Marketing Association Proceedings,* Bernard A. Marvin, ed. (Chicago: American Marketing Assn., June 1969), p. 86.

PART TWO

APPLICATIONS OF MULTINATIONAL PRODUCT STRATEGY

4

MULTINATIONAL COMPANY MARKETING—EXPERIENCE TRANSFER

by Marvin M. Smolan

"Germans are precise, but not creative." "Italians are creative, but crisis oriented." "Spaniards are responsive, but have a *mañana* attitude." "The French must do it the French way." Everyone who has worked in the international operations of a multinational company or lived in one or more of these countries has heard such stereotyped descriptions of the particular country, its management style, and its consumer attitudes.

How does the multinational company market its products when management skills and market behavior differ so greatly? How can the multinational company maintain uniformity and consistency in its product marketing efforts and still provide for individuality in each market? A most important question is: How can the marketing experience gained in one country be applied to a company's subsidiaries in other countries to enable them to profit from this experience?

In an attempt to answer these questions, I will describe here the international marketing philosophy of Schering Plough and particularly our European regional efforts in what we shall call "experience transfer." First, however, I will explain why and how both uniformity and individuality among our subsidiary operations are important objectives of our international marketing effort.

---

*Marvin M. Smolan is Vice President, Manufacturing Planning and Services, Essex Chemie, A.G. (a subsidiary of the Schering Plough Corporation).

UNIFORMITY AND INDIVIDUALITY:
COMPLEMENTARY OBJECTIVES

The first objective is uniformity of marketing efforts by all subsidiaries. This is desirable because of the efficiencies and economies that can result. For example, similar product claims, uniform quality standards, and common marketing strategies allow the cost of developing such programs to be distributed over a number of subsidiaries rather than charged entirely to one.

From the overall viewpoint of International Division management, therefore, it is important to identify the common and uniform marketing efforts desired and to see that these are set forth as division marketing policies and clearly communicated down the line to subsidiary management. It is equally important that subsidiary management understand and carry out these policies. Failure to do this may not only diminish the benefit to the company of such policies, but it is bound to lead to difficulties in properly defining and implementing individual marketing programs at the subsidiary level. Often major problems with subsidiary management have been the direct result of poorly defined marketing policies emanating from ·International Division management or the misinterpretation of marketing policies by subsidiary management.

The second objective is to encourage and stimulate the development of self-sufficiency and individuality in the subsidiary marketing effort. This may appear to be inconsistent with the uniform marketing policy objective, but it is not at all so. Here the objective is to support and encourage subsidiary management, those people who are closest to their markets, to respond to the individual needs of their markets within the uniform marketing policy framework common to all subsidiaries. Product claims or product quality standards may be uniform, but each subsidiary is best able to determine how to communicate these claims and standards to its customers.

EXPERIENCE TRANSFER

In addition to carrying out the two basic objectives of our international marketing effort, a most important role of our regional marketing effort is to provide for experience transfer between individual subsidiary operations. Despite goals of uniformity and individuality, a company that markets its products worldwide and does so at varying times and places must find a way to communicate and transfer the results of its marketing experience from one country to another.

It is particularly essential when introducing a new product that the multinational company establish a mechanism for transferring this experience, that it develop a communication system that will enable each subsidiary operation about to launch a product to benefit from the experience gained by those who are already marketing the product.

What can subsidiary management learn from the experience of others? What, exactly, is meant by "experience transfer"?

Let me illustrate what can be learned from marketing experience by quoting excerpts from a series of recent memoranda between regional and subsidiary managements relating to a new product that had already been introduced into a fair number of markets.

> At this point in time, product 'Z' is available in six markets in the region and has been written into their operating plans for 1975. . . . I am firmly convinced that the estimates for these six markets are optimistic. . . . Additionally, during 1975 a further five markets will introduce product 'Z'. In all cases, I believe the new introductions are also too optimistic, and I have made suggestions for more realistic estimates.

On the basis of this report, individual markets were contacted as follows:

> I have recently spent some time reviewing the sales progress of product 'Z' within the region; and since you will be introducing this product during 1975, I thought you might be interested in the comparative findings. . . . Undoubtedly, product 'Z' has not produced the expected sales that were predicted, and even today the budgeted estimates appear to be on the high side.

A typical reply received was:

First of all, I wish to thank you for the information about the sales of product 'Z' in the different countries. It is the first time I received such complete information on product 'Z'. . . . I agree with you on your advice concerning the reduction to 12,000 units for the first-year forecast and on the strict limitation on expenses; however, owing to motivation reasons, I cannot exclude the field sales force from the product's promotion.

In answer to the specific objection relating to field force involvement, the region responded:

Many thanks for your reply to my letter concerning the performance of product 'Z' in various countries. . . . I do understand that if you are viewing product 'Z' from a motivational point of view, one should certainly consider using the field force. . . . Incidentally, I should point out that U.S. Domestic has now removed product 'Z' from promotion by the field force in the U.S. . . . When you come to the Regional Office, it will give us an opportunity to talk in a little more detail concerning product 'Z'.

This exchange illustrates the way experience gained in several markets was brought to bear on subsidiaries about to introduce the product. The sales history and forecasting analysis were also used to challenge the sales estimates of subsidiaries who already had the product on the market.

Sometimes experience transfer can consist primarily of a case history of one subsidiary's experience. The positive results achieved by one subsidiary may be very effective in overcoming the reluctance of other subsidiaries to introduce a new product. Again, let me give an example from brief communication excerpts. The first is a memo from a subsidiary reluctant to introduce the new product.

Even if product 'X', according to the information available, seems to be highly effective topically with no particular side effects, it does not show superiority that makes it a self-evidently easy task to predict its market potential in a quite developed market such as that of our country.

Now, here are two excerpts from the case history of a successful market introduction of product 'X': the first helped to refute the reluctant country's objections; the second is an example of how regional management stimulates the concept of experience transfer.

It was assumed from the start that the new product would not be expected to represent a "therapeutic breakthrough" vis-à-vis either the existing product or competitive products. This assumption was very willingly revised later, when the clear superiority of the new product became evident!

*   *   *

The case history of this particular country is not the same as that in other countries. The market is different, the organization is different, the medical attitudes are different . . . and many other things. However, good ideas are good ideas anywhere, and good planning in a sound and logical sequence is also international. Hopefully, you have read this particular country's experience with interest and will take what you can use and leave what you cannot use.

Another means of experience transfer, of particular value prior to the regional launching of a new product (before the first subsidiary introduces the product), is the conference approach. This method is used to inform all subsidiary managers at the same time of the experience and knowledge available from the laboratory. Again, let me illustrate using excerpts from bulletins and other communications concerning a new product launching conference. The first is a regional management bulletin calling for such a conference.

A one-day meeting will take place where all these points can be clarified. For this meeting we will have present the technical director and the marketing manager, who will be able to pass on their experiences with the products. Additionally, the medical director will contribute further medical input to the meeting, and all marketing aspects concerning product 'Y' will be discussed.

This is followed by the conference agenda notice:

57

Attached is an agenda for the meeting, plus an updated briefing report that gives the latest situation on product 'Y'. At the meeting, in addition to the medical and commercial aspects of the product, we shall be examining the introduction planning schedules and marketing strategies for product 'Y'.

The third excerpt is part of a memo from one of the subsidiary managers following the conference, in which he refers to a specific market study technique used by his subsidiary to measure the sales potential for the product:

Our study technique has now been translated as was decided during the meeting. I hope that it can be of help to other markets in designing their marketing analysis. As I pointed out at the meeting, one must bear in mind that the attitudes given by the interviewed surgeons are rather divergent and cannot be generalized to too great an extent. Sales statistics and the number of operations are, on the other hand, rather accurate figures.

The next regional management memorandum, directed to those subsidiaries who could not attend the conference, summarized the results of the meeting as follows:

As you have heard, we recently conducted product 'Y' information meeting and, although you were not able to be represented at the meeting, I am enclosing a meeting report, plus the hand-outs and lecture notes supplied at the meeting. . . . Additionally, a presentation showing one country's methods of assessing the market also took place; as soon as copies are available, they will be forwarded to you.

THE MARKETING PLANNING MANAGER

Up to this point we have demonstrated the value of the experience component of experience transfer. But *how* the experience is transferred is critical to the success of such an effort. Organizationally, there is a need for people whose primary responsibility is to ensure that experience is transferred at the right time, in the right way, in the right quantity, and to the right countries. Admittedly, everybody in the International Division participates and contributes to experience transfer. We concluded, however, that in order to make such an effort really pay off, we needed to assign the responsibility for experience transfer to individuals specifically selected for this purpose.

As a result, at the regional level we have marketing planning managers whose primary responsibility is to implement the experience transfer concept. The marketing planning manager's function in specific product groups has been defined as follows:

    a. Provide for uniformity and consistency in marketing efforts
    b. Encourage and provide for individuality and self-sufficiency at the subsidiary level
    c. Facilitate experience transfer between subsidiary managements

To carry out his responsibility, the marketing planning manager must be informed and knowledgeable about all aspects of the specific products assigned to him, including marketing policy, subsidiary management views, and the situations in the individual markets. He has to maintain close contact with International Division headquarters so that he can participate actively in the formulation of marketing policies.

At the regional headquarters level, as a member of the new products team, he informs regional management and is kept informed of new product developments throughout the region.

The marketing planning manager also keeps in close touch with subsidiary management. He needs to know their views and attitudes toward products that are now marketed and those scheduled to be introduced. He must be knowledgeable about the planning and promotional skills available at the subsidiary level. Although the marketing planning manager does not prepare subsidiary product marketing plans, he assists subsidiary management in developing their plans by communicating to them the knowledge and experience that the International Division and the region have had with that particular product.

Although the marketing planning manager has less specific market knowledge than subsidiary management, he can identify similarities between markets that will allow for experience transfer between subsidiaries. He gains this knowledge from market studies, from an intimate familiarity with the marketing plans of the individual subsidiaries, and from his close working relationship with subsidiary management.

As you may gather, the role of the marketing planning manager is extremely important to successful experience transfer and requires a great deal of skill in communications, persuasion, and management, all of which are critically important in this role. As a result, we have selected only high-management-potential individuals for such positions.

PREVENTATIVE MEDICINE

In summary, to successfully market its products in many countries, a multinational company must provide *uniform marketing policies* where needed and at the same time encourage *individuality* at the country level. A most important element of international marketing is *experience transfer* and the means for effectively accomplishing this effort.

Despite the differences that exist from country to country, the experience gained by marketing products in many different markets provides the multinational company with the knowledge needed to enhance its worldwide marketing efforts. Today, experience transfer is equally applicable to the U.S. operations of multinational companies who in the past looked on international operations as simply the recipient of U.S. marketing experience.

In postwar Europe it used to be said that "when the United States catches cold, Europe gets pneumonia." Today that dependence runs in both directions. The same is true with multinational companies: the interdependence of all their markets today, including the United States, demands closer marketing policy coordination and marketing experience transfer.

5

THE INTERNATIONAL EXPANSION OF
U.S. FRANCHISE SYSTEMS

by Donald W. Hackett*

In 1975, the franchise method of distribution accounted for over $158 billion in retail sales within the United States, encompassing a full 27% of total retail sales.[1] This volume of sales is especially remarkable when we consider that nine out of every ten franchising firms have been established less than 20 years.

The term *franchising* has several connotations. For the study reported here, I used Vaughn's definition of franchising as "a form of marketing or distribution in which a parent company customarily grants an individual or relatively small company the right or privilege to do business (for a consideration from the franchisee) in a prescribed manner over a certain period of time in a specified place." This "privilege" may be the right to sell the parent company's product, to use its name, to adopt its method, or to copy its symbols, trademark, and architecture.[2]

The distribution form known as franchising started in Germany many years ago, when beer brewers entered into licensing and financing arrangements for the exclusive sale of various brands of beer and ale.[3] But it is in the dynamic U.S. economy that franchising has prospered. In 1863, the Singer Sewing Machine Company instituted what was probably the first modern form of franchising in the United States; the automobile and soft drink industries adopted franchising as the principal method of distribution in the 1890s, and petroleum producers followed in the 1930s.[4] In 1935, Howard Johnson established the first franchised restaurant chain.

---

*Donald W. Hackett is Assistant Professor of Marketing and Director of Graduate Studies in Business at Wichita State University. The author wishes to thank Wichita State University for the grant that made this research possible.

Franchising in the U.S. began to accelerate in the 1950s. Such diverse businesses as fast-food restaurants, business services, construction, hotels and motels, recreation, entertainment, and rental services integrated the franchise concept of distribution into their marketing strategies. Perhaps the most notable example of the franchise industry's growth is McDonald's Corporation. From 1961 to 1971, the number of McDonald's franchise units increased by an astounding 758%! The corporation began operations in 1955; by 1973 it was ringing up sales of $1.03 billion, surpassing the U.S. Army as the nation's biggest dispenser of meals.[5]

The franchising boom began to level off in the late 1960s. With the advent of the 1970s, many franchise systems found fewer prime locations, increased competition, and an unsettled legal environment. Faced with these conditions, companies began to look for opportunities in foreign environments. As recently as 1969, a survey of the International Franchising Association found that only 14% of the member firms had franchisees outside the United States and many of these were limited to Canada. From this tiny beachhead American franchisors expanded; by 1973, the U.S. Department of Commerce estimated, better than 208 American firms operated over 9,500 franchise establishments abroad.[6] The trend toward international franchising is so well established that it might be described as the second great boom in the history of franchising.

To examine this phenomenon, we conducted a study of U.S.-based franchise firms involved in international operations. This paper discusses that study and examines the results with regard to the major motivations, ownership policies, marketing strategies, profits, and problems of the international franchisor.

THE STUDY

Several previous studies have looked at the efforts of U.S. franchise systems abroad. Walker and Etzel focused on the progress and procedures of U.S. firms operating in foreign markets.[7] The U.S. Department of Commerce periodically surveys American franchising firms to develop statistics concerning their international involvement.[8] The U.S. Department of Agriculture has polled leading fast-food firms to determine their foreign expansion plans.[9] Additionally, numerous "how to" articles have appeared in newspapers, trade journals, and other publications.[10]

The study we conducted examined specific aspects of the internationalization of American franchising firms. Of particular interest to the researchers was: (1) the identification of motivations underlying overseas expansion, (2) the geographic location of foreign outlets, (3) the ownership strategy used in international entry, (4) the effect of foreign environment on U.S. firms' marketing and financial strategies, and (5) the major problems involved in establishing franchise operations abroad.

Data for the study were developed from a nationwide mail survey of U.S. franchising firms. Several trade and membership lists were integrated to form a master composite mailing list; only automobile and petroleum franchising companies were excluded from the survey.[11] Executives of 719 franchising firms were contacted to determine if their firms were involved in international operations. Special efforts, including personal and telephone interviews, were made to insure response from firms targeted as internationally oriented companies. Usable replies were received from 353 firms, for a response rate of 49%. A total of 85 firms indicated involvement in foreign markets and provided the data on which this study is based.

RESULTS OF THE STUDY

A profile of the participating firms is presented in Tables 1 and 2. The respondent firms were classified into nine major categories and then broken down according to when they started their first domestic and first international franchises. The greatest proportion of respondent firms currently involved in international markets, 30.6%, founded their domestic enterprises in the period 1960-1964. Closer analysis of the data in Table 1 reveals that business services and soft drink systems were rapidly developing in the period immediately following World War II. The majority of fast-food, hotel/motel, and car rental firms now involved in foreign markets initially began domestic franchising operations during the 1950s and early 1960s. A total of 22.4% of the internationally involved firms resided in the fast-food group, a statistic that reflects the aggressive nature of these firms in franchising. The extensive involvement of other franchise

63

Table 1

PROFILE OF RESPONDENT FIRMS INVOLVED IN INTERNATIONAL MARKETS:
YEAR OF FIRST DOMESTIC FRANCHISE

Classification	Pre-1940	1940 1949	1950 1959	1960 1964	1965 1969	1970 1975	Total	Percent
Automotive services	0	1	1	3	1	1	7	8.2
Business services	1	5	1	1	1	0	9	10.6
Car rentals	0	1	3	2	1	0	7	8.2
Recreation services	0	0	1	1	1	1	4	4.7
Fast foods	1	3	6	6	3	0	19	22.4
Retailing (food)	1	1	1	4	1	0	8	9.4
Hotels/motels	0	1	1	4	1	0	7	8.2
Soft drinks	3	4	1	2	0	0	10	11.8
Miscellaneous[a]	1	5	2	3	2	1	14	16.5
Total	7	21	17	26	11	3	85	100.0
Percent	8.2	24.7	20.0	30.6	13.0	3.5	100	

[a]Firms classified in this category include laundries, lawn care operations, art galleries, copy firms, real estate agencies, industrial service companies, and nonfood retailers.

Table 2

PROFILE OF RESPONDENT FIRMS INVOLVED IN INTERNATIONAL MARKETS:
YEAR OF FIRST INTERNATIONAL FRANCHISE

Classification	Pre-1940	1940 1949	1950 1959	1960 1964	1965 1969	1970 1975	Total	Percent
Automotive services	0	0	1	3	2	1	7	8.2
Business services	2	0	2	1	0	4	9	10.6
Car rentals	0	1	1	1	1	3	7	8.2
Recreation services	0	0	0	2	0	2	4	4.7
Fast food	0	0	0	5	5	9	19	22.4
Retailing (food)	1	0	0	1	2	4	8	9.4
Hotels/motels	0	0	0	2	2	3	7	8.2
Soft drinks	2	2	4	0	1	1	10	11.8
Miscellaneous[a]	2	1	2	1	4	4	14	16.5
Total	7	4	10	16	17	31	85	100.0
Percent	8.2	4.7	11.8	18.8	20.0	36.5	100	

[a]Firms classified in this category include laundries, lawn care operations, art galleries, copy firms, real estate agencies, industrial service companies, and nonfood retailers.

groups such as the soft drink and business service firms also indicates that overseas entry is an industrywide phenomenon.

The boom in international participation by U.S. franchise systems is clearly illustrated in Table 2. A steady, if not spectacular, entry picture was reflected by respondent firms in the periods prior to 1960; it was in the decade of the 1960s, however, that a major up-swing in international participation evolved. This was followed by an even more dramatic surge in the first five years of the '70s. For example, over one third of the respondent firms launched their initial international venture between 1970 and 1975! Prior to 1960, soft drink and business service firms were the most active overseas entries; fast-food, automotive services, and hotel/motel systems entered inter-national markets most heavily in the 1960s. Since 1970, the penetra-tion of foreign markets has been widespread among the different franchise groups.

As indicated in Table 3, size is a factor in international entry. The systems that completed the questionnaire ranged in size from 21 units to over 5,000 units. As expected, the larger firms ac-counted for the majority of outlets abroad: those firms that ex-ceeded 300 units in size accounted for 76.1% of all international units of the respondents. However, one in five of the respondent firms involved in foreign markets had less than 75 outlets under contract both domestically and internationally. Taking this a step further, 43.5% of the firms involved internationally had less than 200 units total. On the basis of these figures, it appears that large size is not necessarily a prerequisite for global involvement even though the larger firms do presently dominate in total outlets on line.

Table 4 indicates that current operations of U.S. systems are largest in the westernized and industrial nations of the world. Canada has the largest number of U.S. franchise operations, followed by England and Japan. South Africa has an unexpectedly large number of units, but the majority of these resulted from the operations of one drugstore firm. Somewhat surprisingly, West Germany has few U.S. franchise systems in operation, but unsuccessful attempts by two major firms in the early 1970s slowed the industry's move into this market. Australia, Mexico, and Western Europe are also heavily penetrated markets at this early date.

Table 3

RESPONDENT FIRMS' INTERNATIONAL PARTICIPATION BY SIZE

Parent Firms by Franchise Size	No. of Respondents	% of Respondents[a]	% of International Outlets by Size[b]
Less than 49	10	11.8	1.2
50 - 74	7	8.2	1.3
75 - 99	3	3.5	2.0
100 - 199	17	20.0	9.1
200 - 299	14	16.5	10.3
300 or more	34	40.0	76.1
Total	85	100.0	100.0

[a] Read as: 11.8% of respondent firms operate less than 49 domestic franchisee outlets.
[b] Read as: 1.2% of all international outlets of surveyed firms are operated by firms with less than 49 franchisees.

Table 4

INTERNATIONAL LOCATIONS OF U.S. FRANCHISE SYSTEMS

Region or Nation	Operating	Planned[a]	Region or Nation	Operating	Planned
AFRICA			**LATIN AND**		
South Africa	993	32	**SOUTH AMERICA**		
Rhodesia	13	5	Mexico	262	148
Nigeria	9	5	Central America	87	28
Kenya	7	6	Argentina	62	9
Ghana	7	4	Brazil	51	39
Other	32	5	Venezuela	50	10
Area total	1,061	57	Other	78	24
			Area total	590	258
CARIBBEAN	87	34			
			FAR EAST		
CANADA	2,832	932	Japan	1,087	1,609
			Philippines	50	74
EUROPE			Malaysia	41	13
England	1,535	259	India	19	2
Italy	255	19	Guam	18	5
Germany	162	261	Hong Kong	16	8
France	155	45	Other	37	43
Spain	134	32	Area total	1,268	1,754
Scandinavia	101	35			
Belgium	90	28	**MIDDLE EAST**		
Switzerland	71	19	Iran	25	5
Austria	42	7	Lebanon	22	13
Portugal	35	8	Israel	18	10
Greece	28	6	Other	65	28
Other	47	14	Area total	130	56
Area total	2,655	733			
			OCEANIA		
USSR AND			Australia	251	205
SOVIET			New Zealand	44	31
BLOCK	8		Area total	295	236
			TOTAL	8,926	4,060

[a]A total of 32% of the respondent firms intentionally skipped the "planned units" column because of uncertain plans or under a claim of proprietary information.

MOTIVATIONS BEHIND INTERNATIONAL ENTRY

In an effort to identify motivations underlying the decision to expand internationally, we asked each respondent firm to rank the importance of ten motivational statements on a scale of one to five. That ranking is exhibited in descending order of importance in Table 5. Initial entry of most respondent firms was prompted by intermediate and long-run market potential rather than by immediate financial gain. Note as evidence the high rankings of statements relating to market potential, that is, statements 1 and 2, and the lower rankings given to financially related statements 6 and 10. A senior executive's early interest was also a factor in many of the international entry decisions. This interest was frequently initiated by prospective or existing franchise holders requesting rights to develop international territories. Once a system was established abroad, its success acted as a catalyst for further international ventures. Respondent firms ranked the statement concerning a "saturated U.S. market" (statement 8) low in influencing their foreign entry decision. Apparently U.S. franchise systems still view the domestic market with optimism. Few firms credited U.S. government agencies with any meaningful role in their international entry decisions.

The generalization of agreement among the franchisor groups concerning their motivations for entry was analyzed using Kendall's coefficient of concordance.[12] A significant level of agreement (Kendall's w = .84) was found among the franchisor classifications. This extremely high coefficient indicates that the international-oriented franchisors significantly agreed among themselves on the rankings of motivations displayed in Table 5.

OWNERSHIP STRATEGY

The overseas expansion by U.S. systems reflects a variety of ownership strategies. More than 80% of the surveyed companies reported that American ownership abroad is allowed and often times encouraged. This strategy is risky in many nationalistic countries, however; indeed, a number of firms indicated that this policy was under review. The respondent firms were divided on single and multiple ownership policies: for 58% of the firms the international outlets were owned by individual entrepreneurs; for 42% they were

Table 5

RANK ORDER OF MOTIVATIONS UNDERLYING INTERNATIONAL ENTRY BY FRANCHISE FIRMS

Motivational Statement	Rank[a]
Desire to take advantage of market with great potential	1
Establish company name in markets that will be important in the future	2
Proposal from prospective or existing franchise	3
Initial interest shown by senior executive	4
Desire to be known as an international firm	5
Greater ROI than available on domestic investment	6
Overseas expansion of other franchising firms	7
Saturated U.S. market	8
Encouragement of U.S. government agencies	9
Desire to lessen U.S. tax liability	10

[a]The ranks were determined by assigning weights of importance to the individual rankings. The criterion receiving the highest weighted ranking was assigned the rank of "1", the next highest "2", and so on.

operated under multiple-unit ownership. In fast-food systems, however, over 70% of the foreign units were multiply owned.

Table 6 shows that 100% franchisee ownership is currently the most frequently used entry strategy in international franchising: over 47% of the respondent firms used this ownership method. This is in contrast to the trend toward company-owned units in domestic markets.

Table 6

OWNERSHIP POLICIES MOST FREQUENTLY USED BY
U.S. INTERNATIONAL FRANCHISE SYSTEMS

Classification	Franchisee Owned	Master or Area	Company Owned	Joint Venture/ Franchisee Majority	Joint Venture/ Franchisee Minority	Total
Automotive services	4	1	2	0	0	
Business services	5	0	4	0	0	
Car rentals	4	2	0	0	0	
Recreation services	1	3	0	0	0	
Fast foods	7	6	3	3	0	
Retailing (food)	1	2	4	1	0	
Hotels/motels	2	1	0	3	1	
Soft drinks	6	2	0	0	3	
Miscellaneous	9	0	1	0	1	
Total	39	17	14	7	5	82.0
Percent	47.6	20.7	17.1	8.5	6.1	100.0

71

Six of the nine franchise classifications appear to be dominated by the 100% franchisee ownership form. Only the recreation, retailing, and hotel/motel systems used other ownership strategies more frequently. The master or area franchise for cities and nations is the next most commonly used strategy. Some 20.7% of the surveyed firms employed this method; one franchise classification, recreational services, made greater use of this ownership mode than any of the others. A total of 17.1% used a company-owned ownership policy. Food retailers appeared to rely on the company-owned outlet to the greatest extent, while business services and fast-food systems also frequently adopted this ownership form. Several firms noted that new markets are tested with company-owned stores prior to beginning major franchising efforts. Joint ownership positions were the least utilized, with only 14.6% of the firms reporting their use; however, the joint venture arrangement was the most commonly used ownership tactic among the hotel/motel systems.

Further perusal of Table 6 reveals that most classifications of franchisors use more than one form of ownership in international markets. Indeed, ownership strategies are often based on the risk complexion of the nation or region. For instance, since Mexico's passage in 1973 of the Law to Promote Mexican investment, severe limitations have been placed on foreign investment in Mexico. As a result, many franchisors who once wanted to open company-owned stores are moving toward risk-avoidance ownership forms such as the joint venture and franchisee-owned outlets. In Brazil, on the other hand, profits and royalty payments may be remitted only on capital brought into the country or on "reinvestments" of profits derived from such capital. In this case, franchisors often institute company-owned and joint venture operations in order to repatriate profits from the country.

The respondents acknowledged the influence of risks on ownership policies. The driving force behind 100% franchisee ownership, in most cases, was the desire to penetrate markets while avoiding the risks of ownership and financing in the local areas. The master, or area, franchise form was often selected in those cases where simplicity of control and coordination was a primary consideration. Majority joint venture positions were desired by franchisors when the laws of the country required a local national partner and prospective franchisees lacked the necessary financial base. Motivation of the

72

partner, maintenance of some control, lack of available financing, and the desire to reduce equity risk were reasons given for taking a minority ownership position.

MARKETING STRATEGY

Some firms develop unique marketing programs for each international market environment. In contradistinction, other firms institute a uniform or standardized approach to international markets. Indeed, much of the franchising industry's success has been attributed to the predictable nature of product offerings and services. Many franchise systems have successfully penetrated foreign markets with little alteration of the domestic marketing strategy. As shown in Table 7, 41.2% of the firms reported no major changes in their franchise marketing package for overseas ventures. The soft drink, business services, and automotive product groups were the strongest

Table 7

MARKETING STRATEGY ALTERATIONS BY U.S.
FRANCHISORS IN INTERNATIONAL MARKETS

Strategies Altered	No.	%
No change in strategy	33	41.2
Changed product (or service) to fit local tastes	20	25.0
Changed or altered company name or logo	10	12.5
Drastically changed promotion theme	8	10.0
Changed building design	7	8.8
Changed or altered promotional colors	2	2.5
Total	80[a]	100.0

[a]The number (N) on this and other exhibits varies because not every question was answered by every respondent.

73

adopters of the standardized approach, while the more visible retailers were more apt to use an adaptation strategy. The greater alteration of the marketing strategy takes place in the product area. A total of 25% of the companies reported significant alterations of their product or service to better fit local market conditions; however, 70% of the fast-food group significantly changed product offerings in operations outside the United States. The alterations by fast-food groups involved menu additions and deletions as well as changes in aesthetics. For example, McDonald's often uses a heavy wood decor in those nations of northern Europe, such as Scandinavia, where wood furnishings have a long tradition. The alteration or change of logos, promotional and color themes, and architecture was reported by another 33.8% of the surveyed firms.

PROFITS IN INTERNATIONAL MARKETS

As discussed earlier, the motivation for the international expansion of most firms is the initial penetration of potential markets; however, the ultimate success of any business venture depends on profits. The increasingly important role international operations play in the franchising industry's financial posture is revealed in Table 8. The greatest proportion of firms, 46.4%, generated less than 5% of their revenues from overseas operations. Surprisingly, one out of every four firms in international markets already generates 5% to 9% of its profits from these markets, and over 18% of the respondent firms derived 25% or more of their total corporate sales from international establishments. Those groups that began international operations in the 1950s generated the greatest sales from abroad.

The profit-per-unit data reported by the respondents portrays a near-normal distribution. A total of 41.4% of the firms reported international profits per unit about equal to their domestic operations, 31.4% reported greater profits internationally, and 27.2% derived less profit per unit from foreign systems. Within the classifications, the fast-food, recreational, and soft drink systems' profit data were skewed toward greater profit per unit internationally. The automotive and business services, car rentals, and hotel/motel systems reported profits that generally corresponded with domestic systems, while the miscellaneous group's profits were skewed

74

Table 8

CORPORATE SALES GENERATED BY RESPONDENT
FIRMS' INTERNATIONAL FRANCHISES

Classification	Less than 5%	5%-9%	10%-24%	25%-50%	Over 50%	Total
Automotive services	1	3	0	1	0	5
Business services	4	1	0	3	0	8
Car rentals	2	1	1	0	0	4
Recreation services	0	2	0	0	1	3
Fast foods	12	4	0	1	0	17
Retailing (food)	4	0	0	1	0	5
Hotels/motels	2	3	0	0	0	5
Soft drinks	1	1	2	4	1	9
Miscellaneous	6	4	2	1	0	13
Total	32	19	5	11	2	69
Percent	46.4	27.5	7.3	15.9	2.9	100.0

toward greater profit per unit than the domestic establishments. The retailers' profit pictures were mixed, with no established trend.

A profile of the respondents' international sales activities is given in Table 9. Somewhat surprisingly, the food retailer respondents led all categories in number of foreign establishments and total sales volume. The greatest contributor to the retailer category was the convenience food store group; however, over one-half of all food retailer establishments were located in Canada. The fast-food franchisors trailed the food retailers in number of establishments and sales volume even though twice as many fast-food firms responded. The hotel/motel systems, with the least number of overseas units, led all other groups in sales per establishment by a wide margin. Recreational systems registered the lowest average and total sales volume

Table 9

REVENUE PROFILES OF U.S. FRANCHISE FIRMS' INTERNATIONAL UNITS

Classification	No. of Respondents	International Establishments	Average Sales for Establishment[a] (thousands of $)	Total Revenues[b] (thousands of $)
Automotive services	7	1,043	104	108,472
Business services	9	300	61	18,300
Car rentals	6	921	141	129,861
Recreation services	4	108	43	4,644
Fast foods	19	1,367	220	300,740
Retailing (food)	8	1,374	251	344,874
Hotels/motels	7	301	708	213,108
Soft drinks	11	803	N/A	N/A
Miscellaneous	14	2,709	107	289,863
Total	85	8,926		1,409,862

[a] Average sales per establishment were estimated from those firms reporting data in each franchisor category.
[b] Estimates based on "average sales per unit" data supplied by respondents.

of all reporting groups. Nonfood retailers contributed the greatest sales volume to the miscellaneous category, but the heterogeneous nature of this group makes meaningful evaluation difficult.

PROBLEMS IN INTERNATIONAL ENTRY

The problems encountered in foreign markets by franchise firms are similar to domestic business problems, but they differ in intensity and severity. Respondent firms were asked to rank fourteen problem areas on a one-to-five scale. A free-response space for other troublesome areas was included in the questionnaire. As shown in Table 10, host government interference and red tape topped the problem list, followed by high duties and taxes, monetary uncertainties, and logistical, control, and locational problems. The franchisors' agreement on the problems encountered in international markets was also analyzed using Kendall's coefficient of concordance. A rather low level of agreement among the franchisor classifications was indicated by the Kendall's w = .40. Not all franchise systems ranked red tape as their paramount problem. For example, the fast-food group ranked location and logistical obstacles first and second, respectively. High real estate costs, especially in Japan and Europe, created major problems for several of these firms. Hotel systems ranked competition as their greatest area of difficulty, while business and automobile services identified servicing of U.S.-made equipment as the major problem. Somewhat surprisingly, the firms ranked problems inherent in "adapting to foreign cultures" low in the problem hierarchy. Not one firm ranked "adapting the franchise package to local market" among its top five impediments in foreign operations. Governmental, financial, and logistical difficulties were more ubiquitous and appeared consistently as obstacles in all the franchise group responses.

Several problems frequently spell disaster in international markets. Indeed, 40.3% of the surveyed companies reported that one or more of their foreign franchise units had failed. Most franchisors blamed poor management or ignoring established procedures as the cause of failure. Four fast-food systems reported poor locations as the prime factor, while a major restaurant chain pointed to expatriate American managers as the principal reason for its outlet's demise. A soft drink firm and a hamburger franchisor mentioned distance and communication as the main reason for foundering operations, while several

77

Table 10

RANK ORDER OF PROBLEMS ENCOUNTERED IN INTERNATIONAL MARKETS BY U.S. FRANCHISE SYSTEMS

Problem	Rank[a]
Host government regulations and red tape	1
High import duties and taxes in foreign environment	2
Monetary uncertainties and royalty retribution to franchisor	3
Logistical problems inherent in operation of international franchise system	4
Control of franchisees	5
Location problems and real estate costs	6
Patent, trademark, and copyright protection	7
Recruitment of franchisees	8
Training of foreign franchisee personnel	9
Language and cultural barriers	10
Availability of raw materials for company product	11
Foreign ownership limitations	12
Competition in foreign market areas	13
Adaptation of franchise package to local markets	14

[a]The ranks were determined by assigning weights of importance to the individual rankings. The criterion receiving the highest weighted ranking was assigned the rank of "1", the next highest weighted ranking was assigned the rank of "2", and so on.

firms cited the recent economic recession abroad. Finally, one car wash franchisor succinctly stated, "We just didn't do our homework."

FUTURE TRENDS

The firms currently involved in international markets are highly optimistic. They are making plans for further expansion outside the United States, particularly as other economies adopt Western lifestyles and discretionary incomes rise. All the surveyed firms who were active internationally planned to increase the size of their foreign operations, and the majority projected increases from 150% to 300% by the end of the decade.

These plans are illustrated in Table 3 under the "planned units" column. Over 4,000 new units are planned worldwide in the near future; Japan with 39.6% and Canada with 22.9% are targeted for almost two-thirds of all planned units. Germany and, to a lesser extent, Europe, Australia, and Mexico are tagged as major growth areas. Strong interest is being shown in England, representing an area with established trading ties, and the Middle East, a relatively new area of international economic interest. Africa and South America, with the exception of Brazil, are not as attractive to American franchisors at this time. Several firms indicated interest in Eastern European nations, but few had made serious plans for entry.

Firms were also asked to indicate the nations and regions they felt would have greatest growth opportunity in the next five years. Europe was ranked first by 31.2% of the respondents, followed by the western Pacific rim countries, with 24.6%. The Middle East polled 18.6% for third place. But these figures apply only to firms currently involved internationally. Of those firms not currently involved internationally, 28.0% intended to enter foreign markets in the next five years. Undoubtedly, additional franchisors will be encouraged to consider foreign markets as they observe the successful performance of other systems.

SUMMARY AND CONCLUSIONS

The results of this survey show that the American franchising industry is experiencing growth in international markets akin to the domestic market boom between 1950 and 1965. Motivated by the desire to penetrate potential growth areas as early as possible, firms are entering international markets at a spectacular rate. Larger firms,

79

with good profit history in Canada and Europe, have now gained the expertise to do well in more diverse markets and are expanding into the Middle East, Asia, and Latin America. Firms newer to international markets are learning the intricacies of international business and are entering both newer and more established market areas.

In the United States, the ownership trend in franchising has moved toward more company-owned outlets; in international markets, however, the franchisee-owned outlet is the most frequently used ownership strategy. American franchisors do not always alter their marketing packages in foreign cultures; but when altered, most modify the product or service to fit local tastes. Profits from international ventures are mixed, with a near-normal distribution of firms reporting less, equal, or greater profits in comparison to domestic units. Government interference and red tape are the most pervasive problems encountered by U.S. systems abroad; however, the expansion plans of the respondent firms would indicate that these obstacles are surmountable in most regions of the world and virtually all the firms have greater efforts planned for foreign markets. An overall optimism pervades the industry's outlook for the international arena, and greater participation by the industry as a whole seems to be a certainty.

REFERENCES

1. U.S. Department of Commerce, *Franchising in the Economy, 1973-1975* (Washington, D.C.: U.S. Government Printing Office, 1975), p. 5.

2. Charles L. Vaughn, *Franchising* (Lexington, Mass.: Heath, Lexington, 1974), p. 11.

3. Edwin L. Felter, Jr., ed., *International Franchising, Conditions and Prospects* (Denver: Continental Reports, 1970), p. 3.

4. Vaughn, *Franchising,* p. 12.

5. "The Burger that Conquered the Country," *Time,* September 17, 1973, pp. 84-92.

6. U.S. Department of Commerce, *Franchising in the Economy, 1973-1975,* p. 29.

7. Bruce J. Walker and Michael J. Etzel, "The Internationalization of U.S. Franchise Systems: Progress and Procedures," *Journal of Marketing,* Vol. 37 (April 1973), pp. 38-46.

8. For the latest survey, see U.S. Department of Commerce, *Franchising in the Economy, 1973-1975.*

9. U.S. Department of Agriculture, "Fast Food Franchises: Market Potentials for Agricultural Products in Foreign and Domestic Markets," reprinted from *The Marketing and Transportation Situation,* ERS 596 (February 1975).

10. For example, see Matthew Lifflander, "Looking for New Profits Abroad?" *Business Abroad,* Vol. 94 (September 1969), pp. 9-11; and Matthew Lifflander, "So You Want to Go Abroad," *Franchising Around the World,* Vol. 4 (July/August 1970), pp. 24-29.

11. The composite listing was developed from the *1973-1974 International Franchise Association Membership Directory,* Washington, D.C.; the *1972 Directory of Franchising Annual,* Newport Beach, California; the *12th Annual Soft Drink Franchise Company Directory,* 1972, Great Neck, New York; and *The Franchise Opportunities Handbook,* 1973, U.S. Department of Commerce.

12. Sidney Siegel, *Nonparametric Statistics for the Behavioral Sciences* (New York: McGraw-Hill Book Co., 1956), pp. 229-38.

6

GLOBAL BANKING—MARKETING ASPECTS

by Ralph F. Young *

Several years ago, a senior management task force at Bank of America recommended that the bank undertake a major reorganization of its global banking activities. With the bank's rapid growth and worldwide diversification, a need was seen for a structure that would simultaneously permit both sharp market focus and global coordination. A proposal was made to adopt a matrix form of organization that would be "a combination of geographic area operations, worldwide customer and product management [with] multiple functional links between them."

The task force recommendations were accepted. Although there is nothing really new about a multinational corporation adopting a matrix or grid type of organization—a number of companies have been using one variation or another for several years—this did represent a significant departure from organizational norms for a bank.

Initial steps to implement the reorganization began in 1973 and the transition was completed in 1975. Bank of America has become the first major bank to institute a global matrix form of organization with all of its wholesale activities under one leadership.

Although it would be premature to attempt to evaluate the impact on the bank's profit performance of the World Banking Division, as the new organization is called, it might be useful to examine some of the background leading up to the reorganization, and then to look specifically at the marketing side of the new organization.

---

* Ralph F. Young is Senior Vice President, Bank of America NT & SA, San Francisco, California.

REORGANIZATION BACKGROUND

In earlier decades, Bank of America placed emphasis on developing its vast retail banking network in California. The bank's wholesale activities outside of the state of California, where it is headquartered, have only received concentrated effort since the end of World War II.

Why Reorganize? Weaknesses of the Old Organization

National and international operations grew so fast during the past decade that a clear and coordinated effort was increasingly difficult. Structure developed perhaps more as a reaction to current events and needs than by forward-looking design. It was quite a laborious process to develop relevant (albeit sometimes untimely) information concerning the character of business around the world. The result was that organizational structure, and consequently the bank, was not as oriented toward the global marketplace as management would have liked it to be.

Multinational Trend: Overlapping of Customer Responsibilities

Prior to the reorganization, the bank's wholesale activities were split among three divisions—the international, multinational, and national. As the world economy developed, fewer and fewer major corporations in the United States or elsewhere limited business to their domestic markets alone. Lines became blurred. What used to be "national" became "international," or was it "multinational"? There tended to be an overlapping of efforts at the bank as customer responsibility was not always as clearly delineated as it ideally might have been. There was a costly overlap in support functions, too, for each division, and in some cases there was duplication in business development efforts.

Responsibility without Authority

Previously, much of the decision-making authority was centralized in headquarters staff at San Francisco. This staff, in some cases, had little accountability for operating performance or profits. The limited authority of line managers who had responsibility for the operating results and profits insulated the bank from its maximum potential.

Bank Activities and Size

There is a theory that a corporation will reorganize its centralized international division into several area divisions when size abroad reaches 50% or more of total size. At the time the bank's organization was under study, almost half of its total assets were deployed in non-California Division business, and approximately half of its earnings came from these efforts (in the bank's case, "abroad" might mean outside of the state of California). The bank's experience seems to lend support to the structure/size hypothesis.

The California Experience

In 1969 our giant California Division was decentralized into a dozen regional units, and most of the lending decisions were moved out of the San Francisco headquarters. The results in terms of customer service were quite favorable. President Clausen's philosophy has been that directions for profitable growth are to be found in knowing the bank's markets and their needs. He felt that decision-making authority should be transferred into the field near the action to increase flexibility in meeting changing business conditions. In California, this decentralization has been backed up with top management committees that establish and coordinate policies. The chief goal of the world banking reorganization was simple, said President Clausen: "We want to give better service to our customers."

Designing the New Structure: Market Orientation

GM's legendary Alfred P. Sloan suggested that good organizational structure doesn't evolve by itself. Organization design begins with the market. The bank's first step was to clearly identify key market tasks and objectives. The central goal was to make the bank more responsive to customers' needs.

Wholesale customers were classified into three broad groups: corporate, government, and bank. While each individual customer varied in financial need, attitude, and the like, each customer group had worldwide similarities. The matrix form of organizational structure appeared well suited to meeting the dual concern for both sharp local market focus and global coordination of resources.

THE NEW MATRIX ORGANIZATION

Reorganization consolidated all the bank's wholesale banking into a single, unified global entity with major profit centers located in four geographic divisions, as illustrated in Figure 1. The change

Figure 1

CONCEPTUAL MATRIX OF GEOGRAPHIC, FUNCTIONAL, AND CUSTOMER GROUP INTERRELATIONSHIPS

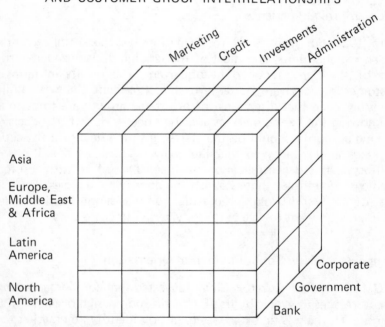

Meshing these three dimensions can be accomplished organizationally by adopting a complex structure such as a "grid" or "matrix." Management's acceptance of this type of structure implies that no single factor—area, function, or customer group—should necessarily dominate in decision making.

was perhaps inevitable, since organizational structure had to be responsive to the increasing interdependence of national markets which, in turn, set the stage for the rapid increase of multinational organizations and activity. The impact of this reorganization for line and staff relationships as well as for overall marketing strategy is described in Figure 2 and discussed below.

Line Decentralization

The adoption of a matrix form of organization had two immediate results. First, geographic line authority was decentralized from San Francisco headquarters to the respective geographic areas. The executive officer with the responsibility for Bank of America business in Europe, the Middle East, and Africa is located in London. The head of the Asia division is in Tokyo; of Latin America, in Caracas; and North America (which comprises the U.S.—exclusive of strictly California business—Canada and Mexico) is now headquartered in Los Angeles.

The reason for this decentralization was to offer better service by having decision-making authority placed in the field closer to the customer's headquarters. Thus, the bank has improved its ability to anticipate customer needs and has succeeded in shortening lines of communication.

Staff Functions Centralized

Second, as administrative and operational authority was decentralized, the bank realized that, to preserve overall coordination and control of the global operation, it would need to group and centralize functional responsibilities. Four senior functional positions were established in San Francisco World Headquarters to help coordinate activities for the geographic divisions and to monitor their performance.

The four functional elements established were (1) Administration (which includes profitability analysis), (2) Credit, (3) Investments, and (4) Corporate, Government and Bank Relations (which exercises the marketing function). It is the responsibility of each of these

87

Figure 2

WORLD BANKING DIVISION ORGANIZATION CHART DEPICTING LINE AND STAFF RELATIONS

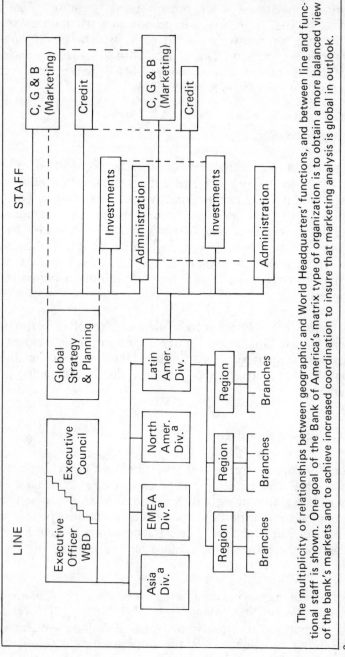

The multiplicity of relationships between geographic and World Headquarters' functions, and between line and functional staff is shown. One goal of the Bank of America's matrix type of organization is to obtain a more balanced view of the bank's markets and to achieve increased coordination to insure that marketing analysis is global in outlook.

[a]These geographic divisions have staff and line systems reporting to them similar to that depicted for the Latin America Division. The same staff setup is mirrored on down through the regions and branches, but at these levels the staff functions are often shared among line account officers so that the line/staff separation becomes less distinct.

elements to assure uniform global policy implementation within its function.

Executive Council: Global Arbitrator and Policymaker

Overall global policy determination, strategy, and planning are entrusted to an Executive Council, headed by the chairman of the bank, who also serves as chief executive of the World Banking Division. The Executive Council has responsibility for allocating resources among the geographic divisions. The council's members include the geographic division chiefs, the functional heads at World Headquarters, and the bank's senior financial officer and the executive officer in charge of global strategy and planning. The council meets at least once a month in San Francisco and acts to achieve balance within the organization.

The council receives strategic guidance from the Global Strategy and Planning Division, whose function is to identify trends before they become generally apparent. This guidance is helpful in enabling the council to foresee opportunities and avoid some surprises.

The "Global Account Officer"

One of the important developments to come along with the reorganization has been the concept of the "global account officer." About 300 of these positions have been created to date, and they are at the forefront of the bank's marketing effort. The global account officer is located in the field nearest to the headquarters of one of our primary corporate target customers. He is fully responsible and accountable on a global basis for service to this multinational client. He has the ability to work horizontally in other areas, as he is assisted worldwide by secondary account officers who may be located geographically near a customer's worldwide subsidiaries.

Several advantages are inherent in the establishment of these global account officers. First, it is explicitly clear within the bank which one person has overall responsibility for a major customer. Second, the global account officer has the time and obligation to become an expert on his client's operations and financial needs.

One of the major criticisms multinational corporations have voiced in the past about their bankers is that they often don't sufficiently understand their client's business and industry. By moving the bank's expertise close to the client's activities, this shortcoming is diminished. The global account officers are situated so that they can become more sensitive to their clients' operations and thus better anticipate needs. They are able to act as financial counselors and to offer specific services tailored to the customer's particular business. Since timing is often important, the account officers have been entrusted with more authority to make decisions on the spot.

CORPORATE, GOVERNMENT AND BANK RELATIONS

The reorganization has generated more than a little enthusiasm and excitement at Bank of America. Much of the interest is centered in the global marketing unit of the World Banking Division—Corporate, Government and Bank Relations (C, G & B), which I head. The somewhat cumbersome name was derived from our three major customer groups: corporations, governments, and banks.

C, G & B is not burdened by day-to-day operational problems, and it is in the unique position of interfacing with many groups within the bank and with the bank's markets as well. This exposure allows a global overview of where the bank stands today and where it has future potential.

C, G & B's role as the global marketing element at Bank of America requires more than merely monitoring the geographic divisions' performance or drawing up policy recommendations for the Executive Council. Principally, the group has a creative function: It acts as a think-tank for new approaches to better serve the bank's markets and helps pinpoint and anticipate customer needs in each of the three global customer group markets.

C, G & B is expected to provide the innovative leadership needed to develop and implement new services to better serve the bank's markets, and to encourage the divisions and individual account officers to accept and modify these ideas as conditioned by their environment. Our group can help line officers market these services to the customers. In essence, our task is to determine what needs to be done to become better bankers for our worldwide customers, and then to assist in seeing that our suggestions are successfully implemented by the line units.

C, G & B Staff: Line Experience

To add the element of realism to the staff marketing function at World Headquarters, officers with line operating experience are chosen. C, G & B comprises former account officers and a branch manager, and their backgrounds are invaluable in smoothing relations between C, G & B and the geographic line in the field.

A vice-president heads each of these three principal wholesale markets. He focuses his attention on his customer group. Our experience has been that momentum is lost, for example, when energies shift between correspondent bank relationships and corporate business development.

Market Integration

Shifting the line decision making to the geographic divisions and on down in the field helps the bank adapt to its external environment. But there are inherent dangers in permitting the bank to become a system of interdependent parts. Russell Ackoff has written that the optimization of subsystems makes it impossible to optimize the total system, and, conversely, the optimization of the total system precludes the systematic optimization of subsystems. The assignment of Corporate, Government and Bank Relations is to integrate the global market activities of the bank so that profits are optimized for the total bank. C, G. & B analyzes each customer group market for market penetration potential and profitability, and then sends its recommendations for action to the field. In cases where policy decision making is involved, recommendations concerning allocation of resources are presented to the Executive Council.

Creative Exchange

The geographic divisions are primarily judged on their profit performance, so it is natural that they should attempt to maximize profits in their defined geographic areas. C, G & B, meanwhile, strives to maximize profits by global customer group, so there is room for a creative exchange of varying points of view. Senior management's decision to adopt the matrix structure meant that neither the area nor the customer group viewpoint should dominate. Both perspectives are important: understanding local conditions and the global overview.

This "meeting of minds" helps insure that a more balanced approach is taken by the bank. The bank's matrix organization permits us to develop global customer group market strategies without losing sharpness of focus in each of the geographic areas. The line is responsible for operating performance, but C, G & B is expected to actively assist in developing a coordinated approach to meet the financial needs of our worldwide customers.

Market Segmentation

The corporate, government, and bank markets are handled separately because they exhibit different characteristics and require different approaches. One of the first tasks for C, G & B was to carefully define each customer group so that each was clearly exclusive of the other. This was not as easy as one might think; for example, does a central bank (i.e., government bank) fall under "governments" or "banks"?

Next we began segmenting each customer group into several parts. Different criteria for each group were used. Size was a critical factor in segmenting the corporate market, while "management style" was influential in classifying the government sector; a dozen weighted variables helped segment the bank market. With the customer markets segmented and targets chosen, the bank has now assigned an account officer in the appropriate geographic division to each major customer and prospect in each of the three major group markets.

Definition and segmentation of the markets was done with the participation and assistance of the C, G & B marketing counterparts in the geographic divisions. Each overseas division has its own marketing function which concentrates its attention on the three customer groups within its defined geographic area. These division-level marketing groups help funnel marketing information from the field to headquarters and participate with C, G & B at headquarters in the effort to achieve overall market integration.

New Financial Service Development

Additionally, we have been delegated the responsibility for expanding current financial service capabilities and developing and introducing new financial service products. Included in this category would be foreign exchange advisory services, domestic cash management services, and an on-line computer data base of both national and international money and credit statistics. The task includes designing the organizational structures and job functions necessary to successfully implement these services. We have found C, G & B to be a good place for this task since it cuts across all the market groups.

THE SEARCH FOR INFORMATION

Historically, the international staff relied most often on informal communications for information. The people overseas and those at World Headquarters knew each other and would communicate directly without strict regard for formal structural lines, which varied according to geographic area. Communication between expatriates in the various overseas units was facilitated by a general camaraderie that developed within the group. This system worked well while the international division was relatively small and almost everyone knew one another.

Before the reorganization, however, there was general agreement that further efforts needed to be undertaken to make the formal system of communications more timely and relevant. Headquarters' requests for information needed increasingly careful consideration, since even innocent-looking requests could prove to be burdensome for the overseas branches.

It was determined that with the reorganization the information-reporting system would be tightened and made more selective. The difficult question was, what information was relevant and necessary?

93

Focus on Market Information

Although semiannual country studies covered economic, political, social, and legal conditions around the world reasonably well, improvement was needed in obtaining marketing information. What was the potential in such-and-such a market? Where was the thrust of the competition? And so on. The field officers were the logical ones to collect basic marketing information, because only they knew both the local scene and the bank's business. One of the primary concerns of C, G & B was to determine what market information was relevant and how the field units should participate in its collection.

Each division and unit was asked to determine first where it was at that point of time in terms of commitments, outstandings, and deposits vis-à-vis each major customer group. The next step was a determination of the size and potential of each market and an estimate of Bank of America's market penetration. C, G & B suggested a list of priorities to be investigated in the field. In the government sector, for example, it is important to know which countries have large funds to offer and under what terms and conditions they will be made available. Which agencies and entities are the attractive clients or prospects? What is the potential of each in terms of financial needs that a private bank could serve? Who makes the financing decisions? By starting the inventory at ground zero, it was possible to expand the listings of potentially profitable relationships in all three customer groups.

This was the first time the bank had conducted such a broad, systematic study to determine market needs and potentials. It was also the first time that focus was placed on each of the three major customer groups as distinct markets. Discovering customer needs would no longer be left to chance. Once customer group market potentials were better known, targets were selected and officers assigned to call on them in a systematic, professional manner.

The Flow of Information

In general, with the reorganization, the flow of customer and geographic knowledge is from the field to a geographic division and then to World Headquarters. There is also a new emphasis on increasing the horizontal flow of customer information between account officers located in different geographic areas. Financial product knowledge, policy information, and suggestions on how to approach functional problems flow from World Headquarters and the divisions to the field.

Although the process is still evolving, the bank's new policy is to encourage a continual flow of current information between units rather than rely so much on the compartmentalized approach of weekly, monthly, or quarterly reports. Timeliness is one goal, but it is also felt that sending current information on a continuing basis will prove less burdensome to the units than the preparation of reports at certain specified periods of time. The advantage for the field units is that they can send information once to a central clearing house (their division and/or World Headquarters), and this information will be sorted there and then distributed appropriately to other units and sections. Before, it was not uncommon for a foreign branch to be required to make up several reports for several different destinations with essentially the same information in each report. The time saved from report writing can now be used by account officers for more direct productive efforts with the bank's customers.

Global Account Officer Information Needs

The account officers not only need better local market information, but they also need to be made more aware of the bank's current money and credit policies, services and programs, and broader money market and industry conditions and trends.

The bank's new computerized system for distributing information has a mailing list of 1,500 world banking officers. Mailings can go to the entire group or to portions selected by unit, by type of job, by geographic area, by account responsibility, or by industry. This is the first time the bank has had the ability to reach specific groups of officers with information that is timely and relevant to them. The distribution system has permitted information to be sent to the field more rapidly and at a lower cost than before. At the same time, information services have been expanded so that more complete information on load and money policies is available.

The bank's Global Business Information System is being developed so that, in its ultimate form, a report can be produced that shows not only each customer's relationships with Bank of America branches throughout the world, but also the relationships of the customer's affiliates and subsidiaries with the bank's units. The system already produces a total-relationship customer income analysis report on top corporate customers that gives the account officer a general idea of a customer's net profit or loss relationship. The report assists account officers in expanding profitable relationships and in pricing new credits (more consistent pricing for multinational customers is a goal).

Each geographic division publishes a newsletter for officers in its region detailing relevant economic and industry trends. Often visiting members of management are also good sources of information.

MARKETING PLANNING AND CONTROL

The line between planning and control activities is difficult to draw since, in many respects, these activities are interdependent and occur simultaneously. The bank's market plans and operating budgets are probably the most important control devices, for they permit a standard measurement of performance against goals.

Who Establishes Market Plans?

In the World Banking Division, we refer to our process as "bottom-up" planning modified and guided by top management guidelines. This is because account officer and line unit plans are consolidated regionally and then by geographic division before coming under review by senior management. With the allocation of resources, based on a scale of priorities, a total corporate plan evolves. This "bottom-up" description, however, is too simplified; Professor Keegan's term *indicative planning* probably better describes what really happens.

There is a dual process going on. Local managers and account officers actively participate and ultimately agree on plans and budgets for their areas of responsibility because they know local priorities and resources best. Reliance is placed on their knowledge about specific customers, what other banks are doing locally, and the like.

The local perspective, however, is not enough if the pitfalls of suboptimization and uncoordinated customer service are to be avoided. A global overview of each customer group and the specific targets is necessary, and C, G & B is responsible for providing this. Our vice-presidents offer suggestions and guidance to the account officers via the geographic divisions. The goal is to push for top performance in each group. The local units, after consideration of our suggestions, draw up their account and country plans according to what they feel is attainable; these plans are then integrated into geographic division plans.

Thus, the planning input is both up and down, integrating both local and global perspectives. Local experience and an estimate of total market potential are the two general factors taken into account. Should there be any significant difference in field and headquarters viewpoints, the Executive Council will harmonize the questions.

The Plan

The evolution of a total plan involves several steps. A "business" plan is developed for five years ahead. The business plan calls for qualitative identification and analysis of markets, including their profitability, the economic/financial/political environment, and the bank's comparative strengths and weaknesses in each market. Goals are set and plans developed to realize the goals. After review, this policy plan is quantified and developed into a financial plan. Simultaneously, a capital budget is developed—on a one-year and a five-year basis—to encompass all projected expenditures. This is an annual exercise at Bank of America, and during the year we continue to evaluate performance against plan. This is especially essential for the World Banking Division, since the global environment is subject to swift changes.

On the local level, each global account officer prepares an account/prospect profile and an account development plan for each primary target corporation. The information includes current business status as well as estimated future involvement, and it is distributed to other officers who might have to deal with this customer in another geographic area.

Control

The decentralization of line authority to the field dictates that the geographic divisions will exercise control authority over the regions within their jurisdiction and the Executive Council will keep tabs on divisional performance. The C, G & B function at World Headquarters monitors field performance with regard to the activities of the three major customer groups. Significant variances from the market plan are brought to the Executive Council for appropriate action.

Although the process is still under development, the goal is to have monthly reports from the local field units comparing the current status of planned goals versus actual experience. This frequency of reporting should enable divisional management and C, G & B to spot potential problems and suggest corrective steps before it is too late.

The C, G & B section is also focusing attention on determining the bank's share of each target market within the three customer groups. This will give management a better idea of where the bank stands competitively, and the information can be used later to compare performance relative to other financial institutions. This would provide the bank with a consistent worldwide standardized approach for evaluating performance in different markets.

We have found that when a staff person is recognized in the field as being the expert in his area, people tend to seek his advice and the organizational flow more naturally passes through him, even if it is not structured formally this way. Consequently, he has greater impact over activities in his customer group market sector. We are now working to develop this expertise and knowledge in each market sector. Travel to the field is encouraged to help the global marketing staff become more knowledgeable about their customer groups, and also to make the field more aware of the importance of global coordination.

OBSERVATIONS AND CONCLUSIONS

The directions for profitable growth are to be found in the marketplace. One of Bank of America's primary concerns when it undertook the reorganization of its wholesale banking activities was to insure a market orientation that combined focus and responsiveness to local markets with a global overview of each customer group market. The matrix form of organizational design appeared best suited to the bank's needs, since the geographic area and customer group dimensions could operate in a fluid manner, without one necessarily assuming a dominant role over the other.

Although it is still too early for us to make any final judgments about the success of the matrix form of organization, profits are up and the direction appears favorable. On the local level there is a new focus on defining, quantifying, and targeting markets, while C, G & B at World Headquarters is now perceiving a global view of spreads, risks, and potential opportunities that will help in coordinating market efforts in all the geographic areas to optimize profit for the total bank.

The guiding philosophy at some of the bank's units before the reorganization was maximize independent profits—finance the most profitable opportunities in your own service area with little consideration of other business opportunities outside of the local market. The bank, with its new global market search, is shifting emphasis from local best to global best in each of its three major customer market groups. The end result is increased global profitability for the bank and improved service for our customers.

7

SOME BUSINESS ISSUES IN INTERNATIONAL MARKETING

by D. R. Cates and C. D. Fogg*

Multinational product management ranks among the top challenges facing businesspeople today. This paper describes a number of practical multinational marketing and business issues experienced by the authors during the past three years. Following a background discussion of Corning's overall international business history, we will identify a number of key issues and problems, discuss their importance, and comment on possible ways of handling the issues or efficiently solving the problems encountered.

BACKGROUND: CORNING GLASS WORKS

Corning has been operating internationally for more than 50 years, but is was not until the mid-1960s that the company made a major commitment of its total resources worldwide. In the mid-'60s a dramatic change took place as a result of management's decision to significantly increase the company's international position by (1) gaining majority control of manufacturing facilities in every important free-world market, (2) placing greater emphasis on exports, and (3) actively seeking license and know-how agreements where it was not possible to establish Corning-owned manufacturing plants.

As that decision began to be implemented, Corning's basic posture shifted, from one of a primarily U.S. manufacturer with limited over-

*D. R. Cates is Product Marketing Manager-International Division and C. D. Fogg is Manager of New Business Development–Electronic Product Division at Corning Glass Works.

seas ties to that of a worldwide enterprise represented in 19 countries with 90 plants, 40 sales offices, 25 manufacturing subsidiaries, and 10 associated companies. Corning facilities abroad can now serve over 85% of the free-world population.

Reflecting this new multinational thrust, sales from exports doubled during the decade 1963-72, and total international sales grew on an average of 20.7% per year, compared to a sales growth of 9.5% annually for the parent company. By 1972, international sales accounted for 28.0% of the corporate total.

At the core of the company's international operating philosophy is the belief that a need exists worldwide for Corning technology and products. Perhaps this is best illustrated in the developing nations, where important long-term needs and, therefore, exciting opportunities, exist, particularly for health, medical, and scientific products.

Corning's International Organization

The international organization has evolved from a small export operation into a separate division chartered as a corporation within the parent company to promote international export sales and to manage operating subsidiaries abroad. With this structure, Corning has achieved rapid growth and penetration in many world markets. Today, however, Corning is in a period of transition and restructuring of company organization.

Various businesses have grown to a point internationally that it is inefficient to maintain major separate organizations for domestic and international sales of the same product lines. Corning has developed a number of worldwide businesses, which organizationally suggests worldwide product divisions. In August 1975, Corning's management decided to restructure this operation, to manage its businesses on a worldwide basis where possible, and to reduce the responsibilities of a separate international division. A key question resulting from this decision is: How should a domestic division and various international organizations be integrated to effectively market a product line? Current reasoning suggests two alternatives. One is a grid organization within which geographic area managers interact with worldwide product managers who integrate all functional inputs for decision

102

making. Another is the total integration of each function—that is, marketing, domestic, and international groups reporting to one functional head. Regardless of the final form of the organization, headquarters should define policy and direction for operational conduct, but it should give maximum freedom to each geographic area to adapt within its environment.

The Electronic Products Division

The authors' principal experience has been in the electronics industry with Corning's Electronic Products Division, which manufactures passive electronic components such as resistors and capacitors. Electronic Products grew from a small department in the early 1950s to a major worldwide business in the 1970s, with a large domestic division and two wholly owned European subsidiaries reporting to a separate international division.

During the 1960s, the European and domestic operations were separately managed and, with the exception of moderate exports to Europe, operated relatively independently of each other. During the late 1960s and early 1970s, the need for stronger coordination of our worldwide components business became increasingly evident—recognizing that, for the time being, the European and export and domestic operations would report through different Corning divisions.

KEY INTERNATIONAL ISSUES

Table 1 summarizes some of the problems experienced or observed during the early 1970s, and defines:

- The areas of issue
- The "domestic only" perspective on the issue
- The international problem that this perspective creates
- Potential solutions implemented or conceived

The remainder of this paper discusses a few of the issues identified in Table 1 in more detail.

Table 1

KEY INTERNATIONAL ISSUES

Areas of Issue	Domestic-Only Perspective	International Problem	International Solution
A. *Charter*	Define goals that direct the actions of the domestic organization to meet corporate objectives in the domestic market.	Conflicting goals such as may be established between geographic areas, resulting in inefficient use of resources.	Establish a charter for all areas to follow in each business or technology and coordinate goals for efficient use of resources.
B. *Role definition*	Define roles that limit the scope of responsibility to the domestic market.	Independent effort often duplicates. Critical interactive tasks may not be accomplished. Economies of scale are not realized.	Define roles that include responsibility for worldwide coordination and profitability.
C. *Organization*	A domestic organization optimizes growth and profitability within the domestic market without regard for other markets.	Scarce resources limit the ability of each organization to satisfy market needs and result in suboptimized growth and profitability for the company.	Establish worldwide organization in each product line which integrates geographic areas, but which maintains identity of different needs and adapts to meet those needs efficiently.
D. *Communication*	Channels and process of communication are limited to the local area of responsibility.	Critical events that may affect other areas are not communicated in a timely manner.	Establish clear channels of communication between areas at each level of responsibility and audit the process to stimulate dialogue.

104

E. *Pricing*

1. Long-range strategy	Establish long-range pricing strategy and cost reduction programs to allow needed profit margin for domestic market.	Overseas pricing and terms are often different from domestic; overseas cost needs may be different.	International representatives participate in development of long-range cost/price plan development. Agree on mutual cost reduction programs if producing in different countries.
		Multinational customers know prices in different countries, will demand lowest multinational price.	Lowest cost/price worldwide must guide process development programs.
2. Short-term pricing (day-to-day)	Establish standard "book" pricing. Special quotes to respond to negotiated business domestically. Apply domestic pricing to overseas export shipments.	For export: Overseas pricing and competitive situation often different from U.S. pricing; costs (CIF) higher; multinational customers know prices for each country, put pressure on suppliers for lowest worldwide price. Quoting overseas business without regard to overseas pricing may result in lost business and profit.	For export: Agree on book prices for international in planning session. Give maximum bargaining latitude to respond to price variations abroad.
			For manufacturing abroad: set price as needed to reach profit-volume goal, and in response to market pricing.
		For manufacturing abroad: Multinational customers know pricing for each country and "local" quotes can be in conflict with policies established in other countries.	For multinational customers: Coordinate with domestic before bidding.

(Continued)

Table 1 (Continued)

Areas of Issue	Domestic-Only Perspective	International Problem	International Solution
F. *Product policy* (new products and extensions)	Establish needed product line extensions and new products by (a) identifying product needs through market research and sales force feedback, and (b) developing domestically. Export what can, without regard to different needs abroad. Product specification, materials, drawings available to overseas ventures, but not tailored to their needs.	Can result in lost export sales, as domestic products in no way tailored to the export market. Overseas, different products or product characteristics are usually needed and cannot be supplied by export. Overseas facilities spend cash to develop a local product that might have been saved by modifying domestic products or agreeing on a standard line to be sold worldwide.	Coordinate product development product line plans: a. Identify products that are common and decide where to manufacture a standard product for maximum profit. b. Identify those that are different and decide where to develop and source them both for local sale and for export. c. Allocate development resources for maximum corporate growth and ROD.
G. *Product Development*	Develop products and extensions exclusively for the domestic market, by a domestic product development group. Ignore overseas and export markets.	Overseas needs often include products different from those needed domestically. Overseas development groups often pursue separate course from domestic. This leads to (a) duplication of effort, as domes-	Identify development needs on a worldwide basis and decide which development groups are best equipped to handle them; tie into worldwide sourcing plan—what products will be produced,

106

			where and why. Establish worldwide priorities.
H. Manufacturing			
1. Development of equipment and cost reduction programs	Develop equipment using domestically available technology at domestic locations.	tic and overseas groups develop similar or duplicate products; and (b) loss of export opportunities, as development groups pursue local products and ignore modifications that might lead to exports. International operation does not benefit from any superior methods developed domestically. Domestic does not benefit from overseas developments that are superior. Each development group not concentrating on developing the manufacturing technologies it is most familiar with.	Reach agreement by all international development groups on what equipment and portions of the manufacturing process will be worked on by whom.
2. Sourcing	Manufacture complete product line for domestic market, expect overseas operations to do same.	Product may not be supplied to the end customer by the lowest-cost, most efficient producer.	Establish coordination between manufacturing organizations to decide who produces what product, taking into account (a) cost, (b) service, and (c) market demand for local production.

(Continued)

Table 1 (Continued)

Areas of Issue	Domestic-Only Perspective	International Problem	International Solution
I. *Multinational contracts*	Domestic quotes based on domestic supply and pricing, ignoring or playing down overseas sourcing.	Foreign quotes in competition and conflict with domestic quotes. Results in both domestic and overseas organizations not providing optimum price-sourcing; causes loss of business.	Worldwide marketing defines key multinational contracts. Key worldwide manager must work out bidding sourcing strategy.
J. *Marketing research*	Marketing research focuses on domestic programs, embracing (a) new products or extension, and (b) customer development targets.	International operations often unaware that research programs are underway. Results in their conducting at a later date, slowing down the development of worldwide marketing and competitive plan.	Marketing activities worldwide agree on key market research program each year. Proceed with research in parallel, where programs have both domestic and overseas significance.
K. *Credit policy*	Domestic organization applies local credit policy for exports.	Overseas credit terms are often more liberal, causing a loss in business if U.S.A. standards applied.	Credit Department evaluates worldwide credit needs and adjusts policy—within reason—to overseas needs (perhaps changing pricing policies to reflect increased cost of credit).

L. *Production allocation*	Domestic organization satisfies needs of domestic customers first.	Overseas demand is not met, resulting in serious service problems and loss of customer base.	Marketing organizations collectively agree on allocation for each area, based on impact on the corporate business.
M. *Advertising*	Media are used for domestic promotions without regard to other areas.	Domestic media with world-wide circulation may be misinterpreted or may convey the wrong message in other areas. Timing and impact may catch overseas organization unprepared to respond to customer inquiries.	Plan campaigns worldwide and coordinate timing of introduction to meet each area need. Use incremental support in each area for reduced cost.
N. *Customer service*	Domestic organization establishes level of service.	Export sales may require different service terms and should be compatible with other area terms.	Coordinate service functions to satisfy each market need.
O. *Experience transfer*	Training programs and personnel reassignment are normally limited to the domestic operation.	Cross-fertilization of ideas and scope of experience is limited. Domestic understanding of the international scenario is limited.	Rotate personnel between areas. Plan and execute joint training, using expertise from each area. Exchange operational "successes" and "failures" to accelerate the learning curve.

109

The Need for Coordination

Separate domestic and overseas marketing and business organizations, with their differing charters, can often follow conflicting marketing policies. A coordinated effort is, therefore, needed in establishing product, market planning, marketing research, pricing, product standardization, resource allocation, advertising, customer service, and training policies, among others.

Communications

To effectively coordinate these policies within the worldwide electronic components business, new channels of communication were developed for tracking projects on a worldwide basis and for the day-to-day coordination required in new product introductions or export sales. Two steps were taken that significantly improved communications and coordination. First, a communications guide that cross-references subjects and functions was developed and circulated in each geographic area. For example, if one faces a customer service problem (order entry, expedites, documentation, changes, invoicing), the guide lists key people to contact in each geographic area and for each product line. An active campaign was conducted to encourage use of the guide, and this tool has now become essential. A domestic coordinating office acts in a backup or consulting role if individuals have difficulty reaching the appropriate people or resolving their problems.

The second step, taken concurrently, was to establish joint meetings of area staff. These meetings are held quarterly and alternate between the corporate headquarters and the area locations. The result is improved dialogue among marketing and general managers, the addressing of key business issues, and the tracking of and measurement of the worldwide efforts. This exchange of information has created an openness that allows effective problem solving to take place.

In addition, a higher level of confidence, trust, and credibility has developed between domestic and overseas personnel. Similar meetings are now being held in other functional groups, such as manufacturing and product development, for the exchange of technical information. We have also experimented with joint sessions consisting of marketing, manufacturing, and development personnel to achieve a cross-fertilization of ideas and problem solving.

Planning

Strategic planning for established product lines and for the development and marketing of new product lines was previously independently prepared by each geographic area and separately submitted to corporate management for approval. As might be expected, each area felt that its projects were the most important; but without knowledge of other area projects, worldwide and regional priorities could not be rationally set.

We are now merging the area plans into a worldwide plan by product line. Product line and project priorities are established on a worldwide basis and requests for resources from the parent corporation are based on these priorities.

Budgets are established and decisions are based on the coordinated plan. Progress is periodically measured against the corrective action taken if tasks are not accomplished on time or if key tasks and due dates are to be changed. Marketing acts as the integrator to guide projects to successful completion.

Pricing Policy

One of the most successful programs implemented over the past three years has been the establishment of pricing policies for each product line in each geographic area. Prior to this, functional coordination did not exist, and each geographic area operated independently in establishing product pricing. Today, we have three basic types of pricing policies, each of which is coordinated.

The first level involves products manufactured within a geographic area and sold in the local markets. The overall strategy is developed in the joint planning sessions for a given budget year. Within that framework, the area organization makes day-to-day pricing decisions needed to reach established goals. The results are reviewed quarterly in the international marketing meetings, where deviations from plan receive special attention and corrective action is developed.

The second class of pricing decisions involves transferred goods. These are products manufactured in one geographic area that are sold to our organization in another geographic area, which subsequently resells the product to the end customer. The local organization acts as an agent or distributor.

For transferred goods, a joint pricing decision between the geographic areas concerned is made on the basis of minimum prices acceptable to meet corporate profit objectives and within competitive constraints. The profit is shared by the two geographic areas involved. This process requires significantly more cooperation and involvement within each market by both organizations; however, the resulting policy is more readily acceptable to both parties and is more effective than a "cost plus" or "domestic price discount" policy in motivating the receiving party to sell the transferred goods.

The third class of pricing decisions concerns export sales direct to customers in other geographic areas. The local organization is held responsible for the marketing and sales decisions in its area. However, the source location establishes the minimum acceptable price on each product. Quite often the practice followed is to extend a contract that exists in one area to facilities of the same customers in another area, with appropriate handling charges added.

Standardization

On the basis of marketing research in each geographic area, we have decided to standardize several products that are manufactured in multiple locations and marketed in all areas. This results in manufacturing cost reductions, product interchangeability, inventory reduction, process improvements, and improved service during periods of rapid growth in demand.

In the past, many barriers existed to accomplishing product standardization worldwide. National identification and cultural pride, combined with a variety of national technical and legal requirements, led to substantially different products in different geographic areas. We have reached the point, however, where cost is the primary factor in many products, so these barriers are being reduced and product standardization is now considered essential to achieving efficient production, taking advantage of economies of scale, and providing prompt service to any world location.

Allocation

During periods of heavy demand, allocation of product shipments has been made to each geographic area to insure that key contract customers, worldwide, are properly serviced. The concept and process were developed in the marketing meetings held to set priorities on a worldwide basis.

Advertising

With rapid communications in a shrinking world, it is essential to communicate and coordinate promotional actions taken in one area to all other areas. For example, if a new product is advertised in the U.S.A., we must be prepared to handle inquiries from other areas based on international circulation of the media, foreign customers with local agents, and the like. This need applies especially to product introductions or cancellations where actions in one location may affect other areas.

Multinational Contracts

The growth of multinational corporations provides an opportunity for component suppliers to meet their needs on a worldwide basis through a single sales contract covering sales from multiple sources. Worldwide contracts offer the multinational firm long-term agreements on pricing, sourcing, service terms, invoicing, and channels of product shipment.

The worldwide blanket contract approach is most effective if the customer is strongly centralized and can exercise control over the remote facilities to purchase on a corporate agreement rather than locally. The logistics of, and need for, coordination between areas on a "real time" basis are significant. Each area organization must provide data on forecasted usage, competitive suppliers, and service needs required prior to preparation of the proposal. This step is taken simultaneously by the customer and the supplier. The supplier must coordinate decision making on the terms of the proposal, including pricing among the geographic areas, and must be prepared to provide local service in each location for the duration of the contract. Timely communication in each stage of the contract activity from quotation to final shipment and payment is essential. Such a total marketing effort can pay large dividends to both customer and supplier through standardized product of uniform quality and design, and economies of scale based on large volume purchases.

Experience Transfer

A joint, quarterly marketing meeting has substantially contributed to an exchange of ideas and practices that can be termed *experience transfer*. This process alone, however, is not adequate to take maximum advantage of the total experience within a worldwide organization. We have found that sharing experiences on major marketing projects is also often fruitful. For example, we recently transferred experience from one area to another in launching a new product. A major campaign was planned, organized, and implemented with appropriate support of sales training, advertising, product samples, and customer contacts, all focused in one geographic area. This campaign was very successful as measured by customer response. In planning a similar launch within another major geographic area, it was decided to use those people who initiated the first campaign in the sales training and initial launch stage of the second campaign. This process proved to be very effective. Preparation time was reduced, most of the aides were duplicated, and the advertising theme was similar.

In addition, we have involved members of marketing management in each geographic location in the planning of business activities of another geographic area. Joint customer visits are made which expose managers from one area to the problems and situations of another. Often these sales calls have led managers to take new approaches with their customers or in their market when they return home.

114

Another common means of experience transfer is through relocation of a member from one area to another. For example, rotation from a regional office to a home office and vice versa.

Training programs can also be multinational. Often we will combine a formal training program, such as electronics theory of our components technology, or our management practices, with a portion of the time used for discussion of company policy, product strategy, market strategy, and pricing policy. The mixing of operational elements into a training program can create additional interest and is an efficient use of the resources that have been committed. These presentations are more effective if made by the business manager of a product line or by the marketing manager, rather than a training director who is not actually working within that business. Face-to-face communication is definitely the best means for the transfer of knowledge; however, many visual aids are appropriate to supplement this process. Videotape has certainly expanded the possibility for primary training and experience transfer to even remote locations in the world. Within marketing, a critique of successes and failures of efforts to achieve new sales and market penetration in one area can guide the organization of another area to adopt the most successful techniques.

Budgeting

The final issue that we will deal with here—budgeting for sales and profits for an international operation—is very important and very complex. One alternative permits each geographic area to independently establish profit goals within that area; subsequent product and pricing policies taken within the areas are directed toward meeting those goals. This can lead to regional decisions— such as a decision to sell local- rather than foreign-manufactured products, or a decision to forego business locally that appears marginally profitable—which do not maximize worldwide profits. This problem is particularly acute when the measurement of success is based on actual cash flows for a legal entity and does not accurately portray the profitability of goods handled by two or more legal entities within the company. Independent budgeting discourages the promotion of sales in transferred goods, thus limiting market penetration and profitability.

A potential solution to this problem is a worldwide budgeting matrix for management control. The process quite simply is a matrix of product sources (all legal entities) versus geographic areas. For management purposes only, products manufactured in one area are transferred to another area at standard cost so that the full profitability of a sale is identified in the appropriate market. The actual transfer price of the sale may then be adjusted for the appropriate cash flow and legal requirements. Results against this matrix budget are reported every four weeks, and analysis of variance is made to determine corrective action.

PART THREE

RESEARCH AND CONTROL IN MULTINATIONAL
MARKETING MANAGEMENT

8

COMMUNICATIONS AND CONTROL IN THE MULTINATIONAL ENTERPRISE

by William K. Brandt and James M. Hulbert *

> There [is] the feeling that the "Multis" make all their big decisions in board rooms in New York and don't take the national interests of their branches here into account.
>
> Ernst Wolf Mommsen, President of Krupp
> (*New York Times*, Nov. 29, 1974)

Where and how decisions are actually made in the labyrinth of a multinational enterprise are questions of continuing interest to managers and government officials alike. Within the corporate walls, sides are quickly drawn in the struggle for power. On the one extreme, we find overseas managers who typically prefer to run their operations as an entrepreneurial venture with minimal interference from the parent company. Managers at headquarters, on the other hand, often feel that the corporation should be run as a global organization with frequent home-office involvement. Politicians in the home and host countries are concerned, but for different reasons. As the "watchdog" or protector of the country's national interests, politicians often believe that where and how decisions are made in a multinational corporation can dramatically influence the economic, social, and political benefits accruing to their constituents.

*William K. Brandt and James M. Hulbert are Associate Professors in the Graduate School of Business, Columbia University. The paper is part of the Columbia Multinational Enterprise Study, financed by a grant from the Ford Foundation and the Faculty Research Fund of the Graduate School of Business, Columbia University. The study is being conducted under the general direction of Professor Stefan Robock. The authors acknowledge the support and cooperation of Professors John Farley and Raimar Richers.

119

Drawing from the results of a survey of 80 multinational subsidiaries operating in Brazil, this paper considers many issues related to these concerns. First, we will describe and evaluate the communication flows between Brazilian companies and their home offices. Communications serve two fundamental roles for the multinational corporation: (1) they transmit knowledge and expertise intended to foster mutual understanding between the two sides, and (2) they facilitate control over local operations. The question of control, or "who calls the shots," in a multinational corporation involves a multifaceted set of issues. These will be examined in detail in the balance of this discussion.

COMMUNICATING WITH THE HOME OFFICE

How does the subsidiary in Sao Paulo or Rio de Janeiro communicate with its home office in London, Tokyo, or New York? How does the home office learn about sales and profit performance, competitive conditions, or problems faced by Brazilian managers? Conversely, how does the home office help the Brazilian company? What kinds of reports, suggestions, or directives flow from the home office to Brazil and how are they used by the company?

On one issue we found almost unanimous agreement: the flow of communications between the home offices and their Brazilian subsidiaries has doubled or quadrupled in recent years. The wonders of computers, satellite telecommunications, and jet airplanes have greatly accelerated and simplified the exchange of information between local and home offices. Despite these changes, there are still problems in collecting relevant, high-quality information; directing it to the right people; and making it useful for decision making. Furthermore, few managers are sensitive to the costs in time, effort, and direct expenses linked to the communications. In this section, we will attempt to measure the communication flows between home offices and the Brazilian companies and to evaluate some effects of the flows.

Types of Communication

Communications between a home office and its Brazilian subsidiary can be grouped into two broad categories: impersonal communications, through regular or occasional reports, budgets and plans, telexes and letters; and personal communications, such as visits, company meetings, and telephone conversations. Whatever their type, communications act as links between headquarters and the foreign subsidiary. These links are more crucial in some companies than in others. For example, if a multinational corporation wishes to integrate or standardize marketing or production on a worldwide basis, substantial interaction is essential. Also, for high-technology and marketing-oriented companies, more information must flow both ways to keep managers current.

Impersonal Communications

Regular Reports to Home Office. Much of the information from the Brazilian subsidiary to the home office was reported on a standardized form weekly, monthly, quarterly, or annually. These reports included statements of profit and loss, balance sheet positions, sales, sources and uses of funds, deposits and loans, exposed assets, inventory positions, production schedules and output, production and marketing costs, and deviation from budget expectations.

Market and sales results were sent home monthly or more often by every company surveyed. These reports ranged from a simple statement of total sales volume to a detailed breakdown by product, market segment, selling price, market share, and expenses. Several American subsidiaries sent reports weekly or every ten days. In most companies, the chief executive reported sales and marketing results to the home office as part of his summary statement or package of reports. In one of every three companies, however, the marketing manager reported directly to the home office.

Financial and production statements were forwarded on a monthly basis to the home office by over 80% of the companies. European companies tended to report financial results less frequently.

Many other reports were forwarded regularly and in various degrees of detail. Among American companies, a favorite was the chief-executive letter, a three-to-five-page summary of activities inside and outside the company, designed to give the home office an overview and explanation of the numerical results.

121

The American Syndrome. American subsidiaries reported to their home offices in far greater variety and with greater frequency than their Japanese or European rivals. Industrial goods companies reported more often than makers of consumer products; otherwise, the major influence on reporting (apart from nationality) was the company's control philosophy, a topic we will discuss later in this paper.[1]

Considering their heavy reporting burden, we were not surprised to find that managers in American firms complained most bitterly about "all those damn reports." Marketing managers in American companies estimated that they devoted 20% of their time to collecting, collating, and interpreting information requested by the home office. This means that, on an average, they devoted one day a week to "keeping the home office happy." In contrast, their counterparts in European companies spent 10% of their time on such duties; and in Japanese firms, only 8%.

Chief executives of American subsidiaries also spent more time on reporting functions. Because many of them began their careers at a time when written reports were the exception rather than the rule, the very thought of reports often caused real frustration. One manager complained: "These reporting forms are so complicated, I'm the only person who understands them down here. This means I spend two or three days every month filling out these reams of paper just to keep people in New York off my back." Other Americans voiced similar criticism, in one case referring to headquarters as the "paper mill." In fairness, it is worth noting that "report-writing blues" were not unique to American managers; several European and Japanese executives were equally frustrated by the heavy burden of reports.

Home-Office Feedback. What happens to the subsidiary's reports when they arrive at the home office? Do they receive careful evaluation and thoughtful response or are they "filed for future reference"? Although we did not measure what actually happened at home office, most managers believed that the majority of their reports were read and evaluated by home-office staff. Somewhat surprisingly, perhaps, those multinational corporations with *more* overseas subsidiaries seemed to do a better job of evaluating reports than those with fewer subsidiaries.

122

It appears, then, that those corporate offices with more foreign subsidiaries must respond by adding staff and procedures to read and evaluate the "mountains" of reports required by the system. As might be expected, companies that were well established in Brazil received somewhat less attention from home office along these lines; however, there was no indication that any one nationality of company was any better or worse than others in this regard.

Some home offices replied to subsidiary reports on a regular basis, while many others followed a management-by-exception policy—becoming involved only when they spotted a problem or an opportunity. Among the Americans, nearly half of the home offices responded each month according to a fixed schedule (e.g., reports received at home office on the third day of the month will be replied to by the tenth). Such a pattern of scheduled responses was found in less than 10% of the European and Japanese home offices, where it was common practice to respond only when necessary. In fact, in some of these companies the practice had gone too far: 20% of the chief executives claimed that they never or only rarely received a reply to reports.

Subsidiary executives criticized both extremes. Managers of American companies generally felt that home-office comments were "incisive" and "useful" but nonetheless complained that "they [home-office staff] spend too much time circling budget variances and asking why." One European derided home-office personnel as "those super-specialized specialists who only see one tree in the forest. As a result, all they do is give us trouble." Timeliness of responses was another criticism: the fact that home-office comments are often elaborate but too late to be useful. One manager commented: "We get this beautiful computer printout showing us where we stand and what to do, but the February results arrive on May 1. By this time we've already corrected our mistakes or we're in big trouble."

In contrast, some managers of European and Japanese companies wished they received more support from the home office. "They send us out here and then forget us back home" was the plaint of these managers, who sometimes felt that their corporation was passing them by. These attitudes reflect more than communication factors, since they may also relate to the company's treatment of its

123

overseas managers in general, including its procedures for their selection, rotation, and promotion.

Reports from Home Office to Brazil. The actual number of reports, brochures, and manuals sent from the home office to Brazil was difficult to determine precisely, but our rough measure showed that American companies sent substantially more materials to assist and coordinate subsidiary operations. Subsidiaries with several divisions or product lines received somewhat fewer reports—perhaps an indication that where numerous home-office divisions were involved, the voluntary flow of information to Brazil was reduced. On the other hand, it could also be that multidivision subsidiaries tended to be more self-sufficient, thereby requesting less information from home office.

Although we did not directly measure the flow of telexes and letters for purposes other than reporting, we observed that American managers relied more heavily on the telex and telephone than their European counterparts. American managers frequently commented that "when I want an answer I phone the boss in New York." Frequently, these calls were to "touch base," as Americans call it, to see whether the home office concurs or more accurately, whether it fails to disagree with a decision well within the authority of the Brazilian manager. In marked contrast to American managers, many Europeans were proud of the fact that they seldom called headquarters. In some Japanese companies, where decisions were still made largely in Tokyo, proposals were telexed from Brazil in the evening and the decision received by the next morning. The twelve-hour time difference gave home-office staff an entire working day to make the decision.

Personal Communications

In international business—as with business everywhere—there are many managers who contend that "there's no substitute for personal contact." Thus, many executives interviewed claimed that no matter how sophisticated the flow of impersonal communication was, personal contact was their most important source of knowledge. This attitude on the part of subsidiary management parallels the feelings of many home-office executives who, according to one recent study,[2] find personal sources of information by far the most important.

Personal Visits. The managers we interviewed spent a good deal of time meeting with home-office personnel. Again, American companies were the most addicted or devoted to the "personal-visit syndrome." Table I illustrates that managers of American companies visited their home office an average of [2.3] times per year. This compares with [1.5] visits for the Europeans and [1.6] for the Japanese.

The same pattern holds for trips to Brazil by home-office bosses. Americans were visited far more often by executives directly responsible for the Brazilian company: 2.7 times per year as compared with 1.1 times for both the Europeans and the Japanese. In sum, for American firms, the chief executive in Brazil met face-to-face with his boss [4.9] times a year, on average, or about once every eleven weeks. In contrast, visits in European firms were exchanged a total of [3.1] times a year, and [3.3] times in Japanese companies.

For second-level managers, the differences were even more pronounced (again, see Table I). Marketing managers of American companies visited the home office more frequently and in turn received many more guests who came to provide marketing assistance.

Why do we find such notable differences in visitation practices from company to company, and what are the aftereffects of the visits? Besides the nationality differences, one factor stands out: the number of visits is directly related to the size and complexity of the parent company. Thus, as companies grow and establish more overseas subsidiaries, such visits become more frequent.

An economy-of-scale factor probably operates in favor of the larger companies, making it more efficient and economical to visit several subsidiaries on one overseas trip. Furthermore, larger corporations generally devise elaborate and multilayered organizational structures, which means that impersonal communications are filtered and delayed. Personal visits can break these bottlenecks and facilitate faster information flow with less misunderstanding.

Table 1

PERSONAL VISITS BETWEEN SUBSIDIARY AND HOME OFFICE

A. Visits between Chief Executive in Brazil and Home-Office Superiors—Median Visits per Year

Nationality of Parent Company	To Home Office by Chief Executive	To Brazil by Home-Office Superiors	Total Visits	Number of Companies
American	2.2	2.7	4.9	(24)
European	1.5	1.1	3.1	(28)
Japanese	1.6	1.1	3.3	(11)
Average for all companies (Total)	1.8	1.4	3.6	(63)

B. Visits between Marketing Manager in Brazil and Home Office Superiors—Median Visits Per Year

Nationality of Parent Company	To Home Office by Marketing Manager	To Brazil by Home-Office Superiors	Total Visits	Number of Companies
American	1.5	5.6	7.1	(29)
European	.7	1.3	2.3	(25)
Japanese	.3	1.5	1.5	(8)
Average for all companies (Total)	.9	2.3	3.4	(62)

126

Size alone, however, is not the only influence on visitation patterns—or why American multinational corporations rely on them so heavily. Some have suggested, for example, that because Brazil is so important to American multinational corporations, their home offices watch it closely. Yet, Brazilian sales as a percent of world sales are higher on average for the Europeans (3.6%) than for the Americans (2.1%). Given these figures, why aren't European home offices watching Brazil even more closely? Further, time-zone changes between Brazil and the home offices, which make visits more fatiguing, are not drastically different for European (four hours) or American (one to four hours) companies. It is our conclusion—to be developed later—that such intensive visitation patterns are part of an extensive and formal control system adopted by many American companies.

We do know, however, that not all such visits to and from Brazil are effective. To be successful, personal visits require homework and planning by home-office and subsidiary personnel. Too often neither is done sufficiently and the visits accomplish little. Key personnel or relevant data are unavailable and decisions must be postponed. On other occasions, the home-office executive is making a "whistle stop" tour of Latin America, which after the second or third country becomes rather ineffectual.

Although a few European executives still wish to see their home-office superiors more often, many European and American managers suffer from overvisitation. "We've been discovered," complains one manager. "Every year between December and March, when it's cold in New York, we're overrun with visitors." One company, which in one year hosted nearly 400 "official" visitors from home office, now requires approval from the subsidiary before a visit can be made. Other companies are following this practice to reduce "vacation" visits, and some even require a visit evaluation before the visitor leaves the country. We wish to qualify that we are not underestimating the value of purposeful face-to-face conversations between home-office and Brazilian managers. Our main concern is that these visits frequently become perfunctory, carried out because "it's time we see what's going on in Brazil," not for any pressing need. Both sides certainly gain something from such visits, but at what cost in terms of managerial time, energy and direct expenses?

127

Company Meetings. In addition to personal visits, over half of the companies interviewed reported holding regular meetings during which subsidiary managers confer with regional or home-office personnel for two to three days. The rationale behind such meetings is simple: they offer opportunities through lectures and workshops to communicate company goals and strategies, to unveil new products and technology, and to interact with other managers and home-office personnel. In some companies, these meetings were held for the Latin American region; in others, for product divisions; and in others, for subsidiary managers worldwide.

American companies held these management conferences far more frequently than either the Europeans or the Japanese. Most of the manager meetings included the chief executives from all worldwide subsidiaries, but a number of American companies were moving to both worldwide and regional meetings on a annual basis. Besides nationality differences, an important influence on whether a company held such meetings was the number of subsidiaries managed by the multinational corporation. As the network of overseas affiliates grows, the company conference becomes more efficient as a means of communicating corporate goals, strategies, and programs for the coming year.

Nearly two thirds of the American parent companies also held meetings specifically for their marketing managers, a practice far less common in European and Japanese companies.

Several non-American managers lambasted the practice of regular meetings, one Japanese saltily reporting, "No, we don't have any jamborees . . . we used to, but we found them a waste of time." Another hard-bitten European chided the Americans for their "Annual World Christmas parties."

Certain industries, such as pharmaceuticals and domestic appliances, tended to hold more regional marketing meetings. For these products, the home office became more involved in marketing activities and apparently found it more efficient and effective to call a meeting to present the annual program. When the Brazilian subsidiary represented a larger share of world sales, however, its managers were less inclined to attend corporate or regional conferences.

EFFECTS OF COMMUNICATIONS

Does Home Office Understand?

How do reports, visits, conferences, and other communications influence the working relationships between home-office and Brazilian management? Do communications enhance understanding or does the burden of reports and meetings lead to frustration and dissension? Our survey included a question that asked subsidiary executives how well they thought the home office understood their problems in Brazil. Nearly half believed that in general their home office understood their situation very well. Nonetheless, one out of four believed that his home-office superiors and staff did not comprehend his problems in Brazil.

What kinds of companies were noted for better or worse understanding? Managers of Japanese companies, in particular, felt that their home offices had a poor understanding of what was going on in Brazil. Indeed, several claimed that home-office relations posed bigger problems than relations with the Brazilian government or personnel problems within the subsidiary.[3] When we consider that many of the Japanese companies had entered the Brazilian market rather recently, this finding is not surprising. In overseas manufacturing, most Japanese multinationals were newcomers compared to their European and American competitors. "We are still learning," claimed one executive. "Twenty-five years ago we knew very little about exporting and we learned. Now we have to learn how to manufacture outside of Japan and Southeast Asia." The sharp cultural differences between Japan and Brazil make the transition more difficult, but companies with a longer tenure in Brazil appear to have solved these problems reasonably well. One manager warned, however, that the contrasting time perspectives of the Japanese and Brazilians may lead to serious frustrations, particularly in joint-venture operations. "It's like sitting at opposite ends of a table. The Brazilians are in a hurry; they want profits now. We're in less of a hurry; we're willing to take our time with profits."

Besides the Japanese influence, we also found that companies with high capital intensity, which requires close home-office involvement, enjoyed better understanding as a result. Decisions to invest large amounts of capital demand extensive planning and monitoring;

129

such attention tends to enhance home-office comprehension of the overseas situation.

One might expect that companies that are more "international" would also have a better understanding, yet the results did not support this idea. Neither the parent company's size nor its proportion of overseas sales was associated with how well the home office was thought to understand the situation in Brazil. The sales volume in Brazil also had no effect on understanding, but product-line complexity was important. Executives of more diversified firms perceived less understanding at home office. This is because as more people (divisions) become involved at home office to provide technical and product support, the likelihood of confusion, bottlenecks, and misunderstandings also increases.[4]

A rather surprising result showed that the quantity of communications—number of reports, personal visits, or conferences—had no substantial effect on perceived levels of understanding. What was done with those reports did seem important, however: if the subsidiary manager believed that his reports were being carefully read and evaluated, he also felt that the home office better understood his problems.

Who Wants More Information?

Despite the fact that virtually no one wished to send more information *to* the home office, one of every three executives wanted help *from* the home office. Some wanted very specific information:

- What's going on in world markets?
- How will regional or worldwide economic and political conditions affect our markets?
- What's happening to sister subsidiaries who might be manufacturing and selling similar products?
- What marketing strategies have succeeded or failed elsewhere?
- What technical problems might be encountered with a new product or process?

Others simply wanted to participate more in the corporate family circle, to feel less isolated from sister subsidiaries and the home office. Some European executives claimed that they learned more

130

from home-country bank representatives than from their home office. Regardless of details, most executives were seeking better-quality information rather than greater quantity. Illustrating this dilemma, one manger quipped: "I've already taken two speed-reading courses to keep up with all these reports. What I really need is some way to wade through the 90% of irrelevancies and spot the 10% that's useful."

Despite some company-by-company differences, a number of generalizations are important. Firms requiring a lower capital intensity such as food or pharmaceutical manufacturers—which tended to enjoy lower levels of home office understanding—were the most eager for additional information from office.

Companies headed by Brazilian nationals also wanted more support from home office. These managers were generally less familiar with home-office policies and politics and therefore were forced to rely on "proper channels" to acquire the desired information. Since these channels were often filtered or blocked, the manager became frustrated in his quest for help. As companies hire more nationals for top management positions, the seriousness of this problem is likely to grow.

Among those companies not desiring more information were those receiving regular feedback from home office. This may reflect an *après le deluge* response for, as one manager commented, "Home office doesn't always send the help we need, but we certainly don't want any more reports or guidelines; we can't read all we receive now." Others also noted that when home office responds to every detail, a practice labeled "variance circling" by some executives, the feeling of being scrutinized can elicit resentment toward any form of home-office "intrusion," whether it is helpful or not. Thus, excessive feedback may lead to a backlash response that causes managers to react against home-office information—even though they might in fact need assistance.

Suggestions for Change

A few summary comments may help clarify the issues raised by this discussion. First, better understanding between home offices and Brazilian companies may be important for reasons besides maintaining smooth working relationships. For example, companies with better home-office understanding also tended to perform better in terms of return on investment. Many other factors also relate to performance, but support and understanding from the home office should not be overlooked as a positive influence.

Throughout our interviews it became clear that many companies were searching actively for a communications system that would meet their needs for timely and accurate information. The prevailing attitude in many American companies was that "more is better": when in doubt, send all the information. This burdens the user with the problem of sifting and sorting to find the useful data; and, as we have already noted, this system adds little in terms of improving understanding between home office and the subsidiary. In contrast, the thinking in some European companies was quite the opposite: send nothing unless it is requested and even then don't be in a hurry about it. Such practices waste time and often lead to decision making based on limited information.

For most companies in the sample, the need for improved communications was strong. Relevancy and quality of information are key criteria too often ignored in the standardized reporting systems of many companies. Under pressure to fill the blanks on the reporting form, concern for data quality takes a back seat. It may be true that numerical "guesstimates" are better than no information at all, but in the extreme such exercises make a charade of management decision making. Managers at home office and in Brazil need to sit down and decide together what information both sides need, how good the data must be, how often the figures should be reported, and who should be responsible for collecting and interpreting the information. We recognize that a multinational corporation operating in 60 nations cannot develop a unique system for each market, but within a standardized system some adjustments and deviations can be tolerated.

Furthermore, too often a random request for specific data in one market gets locked into the worldwide reporting system, never to be questioned again as to why it is there or what purpose it serves. A brief anecdote by a high-ranking executive at one home office illustrates this phenomenon:

132

Several years ago our company president was asked about the market share for a minor product in Helsinki, Finland. When he learned that no one at home office knew the answer, he demanded that henceforth every overseas subsidiary would report market share figures monthly, broken down by market segments for all products. While this may be a simple exercise in the U.S., it's hardly an easy task in Peru, Thailand, or most of the other forty-plus markets we operate in. Nonetheless, we now receive market share data each month—we know it's garbage and the subsidiaries know it, too, but we continue to play the game. Please don't ask me how much it probably costs us each year.

Facilitating understanding and coordination was not the only reason for the heavy communication flows observed in many companies. In fact, the previous analysis suggests that the quantity of communications has comparatively little impact on how well home office is perceived to understand the subsidiary. In most cases, we concluded that home-office control over subsidiaries was a major purpose of communications, an hypothesis that we will now examine.

HOME-OFFICE CONTROL

It is axiomatic that any international firm must exert some kind of control over its subsidiary operations; in the absence of such control, one could argue that it makes more sense to talk of a collection of individual entities. How the parent companies choose to exercise their control, however, is truly multifarious. Control can range from minimal involvement, where the home office intervenes only after several years of heavy losses, to direct involvement in virtually all subsidiary decisions via elaborate communication/reporting systems and rigid budgetary/policy guidelines. Between these extreme positions there are many others, each with its own consequences in terms of costs of operation, flexibility, loyalty, and motivation of subsidiary personnel, to name a few.

In this section, we will examine how companies divide the decision-making power between the home office and Brazil, and will point out some of the advantages and drawbacks of the various approaches. To begin, we will consider some of the obvious differences associated with the nationality of the parent company.

Differences Associated with Nationality Group

Budgetary Limits. Since chief executives like to be relatively autonomous, with broad decision-making authority, the issue of budget guidelines had to be approached with some delicacy. Contrary to their initial comments, it often turned out that the managers were free to make expenditures only if they were previously included in the operating plan or capital budget, which had been approved by the home office. In some companies, these expenditures were approved *en bloc* with allocations that were not binding, thereby granting considerable discretion to the subsidiary executive. In other companies, allocations were proposed and approved on a case-by-case basis; and in still others, the manager had nominal discretion but was unwilling to exercise it without prior approval from his home office.

To gain a clearer idea of the chief executive's budgetary authority, we asked the following question:

> Suppose that during the operating period—after plans have been developed and approved—some kind of emergency arises which requires you to make an expenditure which was not foreseen in the plan or budget. How much could you spend without having to seek prior approval from home office?

In these terms, Table 2 illustrates quite clearly that subsidiary managers in American and Japanese companies had much tighter restrictions than the Europeans. In two thirds of the respondent American and Japanese companies, the chief executive was constrained by a $5,000 ceiling. Such a limit was found in only one fourth of the European companies.

Within each nationality group, we found a number of unusual cases that mitigate against any sweeping conclusions. In at least two European companies, the manager was constrained by a $1,000 limit; on the other hand, a few managers of American companies "ran their own ship" with little home-office intrusion of any kind. In general, however, the European companies enjoyed the most budgetary discretion; though few could match the elfish glee of one

134

Table 2

BUDGETARY LIMIT FOR CHIEF EXECUTIVES BY NATIONALITY OF PARENT COMPANY

Nationality of Parent Company	Less than $5,000	$5,000–$49,999	$50,000–$500,000	No Effective Limit	No. of Companies
American	67%	23%	5%	5%	(21)
European	27	9	41	23	(22)
Japanese	67	0	0	33	(9)
Average for all companies (Total)	50%	13%	19%	17%	(52)

European manager who, while showing us his factory, pointed out a $250,000 piece of automated equipment and remarked, "They [home office] don't even know I have that yet . . . ."

Freedom to Make Decisions. How much freedom do subsidiary executives have to make day-to-day management decisions? A personal pride that "I'm the real boss" is bound to bias answers in the direction of greater freedom, a bias that is likely to occur regardless of nationality. Here again we find that managers of European firms indicated far more freedom to make day-to-day decisions. The sharpness of this distinction supports the findings we observed for spending limits and the overall pattern of tighter home-office control in American companies observed throughout the study.

In what areas do subsidiaries have the least freedom? As one might expect, chief executives of all nationalities reported the least freedom in financial decisions. A tight rein on the purse strings seems to be a characteristic shared by all multinationals; though, as we saw in Table 2, a "tight rein" must be defined in relative terms. Marketing enjoyed the most freedom from home-office controls, with production falling somewhere between the two.[5]

Evolution of Management Control

Current Trends. The discussion to this point has presented a rather static picture of what is happening today and some of the reasons why. We observed consistent and important differences in management practices among companies, particularly among nationality groups; but what explains these differences and what changes might be expected in the future?

Nearly half of the managers interviewed believed that their overall freedom to make decisions had increased during the past five years (Table 3). Part of this feeling may be attributed to the manager himself—as he gains experience and tests the limits of his authority, he begins to perceive that his autonomy has increased. On the other hand, one fourth of the managers felt that home-office reins had tightened. What make these findings interesting are the differences among nationalities. For the Europeans there was a clear trend toward greater freedom; for the Japanese, somewhat less so; and for the Americans, the results were on a toss-up, with 36% reporting more freedom and 36% perceiving less.

136

Table 3

CHIEF EXECUTIVES' PERCEPTIONS OF CHANGES IN FREEDOM TO MAKE DECISIONS

Nationality of Parent Company	During Past Five Years, Decision-Making Freedom Has—				No. of Companies
	Increased	Remained Unchanged	Decreased	Total	
American	36%	28%	36%	100%	(14)
European	55	30	15	100	(20)
Japanese	42	29	29	100	(7)
Average for all companies (Total)	44%	29%	27%	100%	(41)

Note: This question was asked only of managers who had been subsidiary chief executives with the parent company, in Brazil or elsewhere, for at least five years.

Two Approaches to Control. What explains these apparent trends? Why are some companies shifting in one direction and others in the opposite? To help find some answers, we examined two major approaches to administrative control: centralized and bureaucratic.

With a centralized approach, the power to make decisions is restricted to managers at more senior levels in the organization. There is less need for communications and control procedures, since decisions are made by a small group at the top. Policy guidelines dealing with planning, budgeting, and reporting are reduced, as is the infrastructure of staff personnel used to handle these matters. Senior managers keep their eye on the various operations, and when attention is required they get involved directly.[6]

At the other extreme, a bureaucratic approach controls decisions more indirectly by relying on procedures and guidelines. Lower-level managers are free to make decisions, but only within prescribed limits. Planning, budgeting, and reporting procedures are well laid out and generally consistent for many or all groups within the organization. More people are involved, directly or indirectly, in the decision making, many with the control system itself. Senior-level managers are free to intervene in decisions, but typically they practice management by exception—becoming involved upon the request of lower-level managers or when limits or procedures are violated.[7]

Translating theory into variables that are measurable is difficult and imprecise at best; nevertheless, we have attempted to identify which companies seemed to fit into each category. Using two variables relating to bureaucratization and centralization, we created the two-by-two matrix shown in Figure 1, after which we classified each company into one of the four cells.

To measure the degree of direct intervention by home office, we focused on the number of personal visits to Brazil by executives at home office who were superior to the subsidiary chief executive. The other dimension considered the extent to which managers were required to conform to a common format developed by home office when planning and reporting about their operations. A cut-off point was selected, and two categories were created for each variable.

In theory, Cells I and III are consistent with the two approaches described above, Cell I typifying the highly centralized company and

138

Figure 1

ADMINISTRATIVE CONTROL MATRIX

Degree of Home-Office Intervention via Personal Visits to Brazil	Extent of Formalized Planning and Reporting Procedures	
	Less Formal	Formal
Few Visits	II Laissez Faire	III Decentralized Bureaucracy
Many Visits	I Centralized	IV Centralized Bureaucracy

Cell III representing the decentralized firm. Cells II and IV represent approaches that, on the surface at least, seem inconsistent with the two extremes. We call these "laissez-faire" companies (II) and "centralized bureaucracies" (IV).

Classifying the Companies. The 59 companies for which data were available were classified as follows:

Cell	Description	No. of Companies
I	Centralized approach	3
II	Laissez faire	11
III	Decentralized bureaucracy	29
IV	Centralized bureaucracy	16

What kinds of companies fell into each category? Four conditions seemed to explain in large part where the companies were located in the matrix:

139

—Worldwide sales of parent company
—Number of countries with manufacturing subsidiaries
—Sales of Brazilian company
—Nationality

For the first three measures the patterns observed in Table 4 are entirely consistent. In each case, the companies in Cell I were the smallest in terms of subsidiaries and sales in Brazil and world sales. The laissez faire companies (II) were second smallest, followed by those with decentralized bureaucracies (III) and, finally, the centralized bureaucracies (IV). Companies in Cell I were exclusively European; in Cell II, predominantly European; in Cell III, a mixture; and in Cell IV, largely American.

Thus, we see that the size of the world corporation, in terms of sales volume and number of foreign subsidiaries, represented the driving force toward a standardized planning and reporting format. The same conditions operate in favor of a more decentralized organizational structure.

Companies in Cell IV are the so-called "global" corporations, with operations stretching around the world. In fact, many of these companies attempt to plan and develop strategy on a global basis, which in turn demands a higher level of integration between home offices and their subsidiaries. This was demonstrated in several ways. Centralized bureaucracies filed far more reports each month than any of the other types, suggesting that communications serve not only to coordinate, but also to control the foreign affiliate. Managers of these companies also reported less autonomy to make decisions, again characterizing tight integration and control.

Control: Some Warnings

Having considered the types of control used by companies and what is likely to occur in the future, we turn now to some of the unexpected consequences of control strategies. Whenever controls are placed on managers or a system, two types of results can occur—those intended or those unexpected (and generally undesirable). Because the unexpected results typically increase as controls are added, the issue of how much control should be exercised requires

140

Table 4

CHARACTERISTICS OF COMPANIES BY CONTROL CATEGORY

Characteristics	I Centralized	II Laissez Faire	III Decentralized Bureaucracy	IV Centralized Bureaucracy
World sales[a]	935	1,156	3,096	6,126
Number of subsidiaries	8.5	12.2	19.4	29.7
Brazil sales	25.3	42.2	92.6	99.3
Nationality				
% American	0	9	31	75
% European	100	64	48	13

[a]All sales figures are for 1972, in millions of U.S. dollars.

a delicate balance. Unfortunately, in some corporations, the lessons preached for years by sociologists and others who studied this trade-off have apparently been forgotten. Signs of unintended consequences were particularly evident in two areas, as discussed below.

Circumventing the Limit. Setting a reasonable expenditure limit for subsidiary managers depends on a variety of factors: type of industry, subsidiary size, corporate philosophy, and type of decision, to name a few. It would be naive, therefore, to advocate any particular figure for all companies. Nevertheless, if subsidiary managers feel that the limit is too low or that the home office will not listen to reason, they typically practice what is known as "limit avoidance." Using such a guise, a manager faced with a discretionary limit of $5,000 who wishes to make a larger expenditure simply records the expenditure in two, three, or more components, each below the mandatory limit. Although this kind of avoidance is better than complete concealment, and good auditing should detect such behavior, the more important question is whether the limit is appropriate or reasonable. For example, in a subsidiary with $50 million in sales, a budget limit of $1,000 or less for unbudgeted items hardly fits with the notion of decentralization, which the company espouses. In reality, we suspect that such control policies are seldom reviewed and, given the explosive growth of some subsidiaries, these policies soon become outdated.

The Pressure Cooker Problem. Elsewhere we have elaborated on the finding that for American companies the plan typically represents a commitment rather than a coordinating device as used in other multinationals.[8] If the pressure to meet these objectives becomes excessive, distortion is inevitable.[9] First and foremost, budgets or plans provide standards (albeit imperfect) for evaluation; they are not primarily pressure devices. Finding themselves inescapably caught in such "pressure cooker" situations, subsidiary managers respond predictably by doing everything possible to meet those targets. In its simplest form, this involves period-to-period manipulation of sales revenues and costs in order to "hit that bottom line," a practice openly admitted to in several subsidiaries. More complex schemes completely conceal the true picture from home office by preparing different sets of books: one for home office, one for the government, and a third for subsidiary managers. Such a response largely defeats the purpose of the corporate planning process. How

142

much pressure should be applied to meet the planning targets is not a simple question, but the dangers of too much pressure are becoming painfully apparent to some multinationals.

SUMMARY

This paper has examined the interrelated issues of communications and control. In terms of communication flows between home-office and subsidiary managers, the American multinationals ranked highest on every measure. The Europeans maintain much looser linkages with home office and, with some notable exceptions, communicate far less frequently than their American counterparts. The Japanese, still new to overseas manufacturing, fall somewhere between the Americans and the Europeans as they seek to develop communications systems that best meet home-office and subsidiary needs. In Brazil, at least, the Japanese still face serious problems getting their home offices to understand the local environment.

Besides the influence of nationality differences, other conditions appeared to be impelling companies toward a more structured and formal system of communications. With greater commitment to foreign business—as measured by the number of countries in which the company manufactures and the volume of world sales outside the home market—the corporation increases its reliance on personal visits and conferences, together with more rigid reporting procedures.

This pattern fits the American inclination toward more structure and system, but what about the Europeans? What happens as their subsidiary network expands and the need increases to integrate planning and resource allocation on a worldwide basis? Some of the Europeans appear to be moving or have already moved to a more structured "American-style" system, while others with heavy overseas involvement are resisting this change—preferring instead to use more expatriates from the home office to manage their Brazilian operations. Still others appear to be less concerned about worldwide integration and will probably continue to treat their subsidiaries as autonomous affiliates, with relatively little need for tighter linkages with the home office.

One particularly interesting finding is that the *volume* of communications by itself makes little difference in terms of how well the home office is perceived to understand subsidiary problems. Not the number of reports, or of personal visits, or of conferences has any significant impact on understanding as perceived by subsidiary managers.

WHAT CAN BE DONE

Effective communications require cooperation and adaptability on the part of subsidiary and home-office managers. Home-office executives and staff must recognize the time and manpower constraints at the subsidiary level. Often the data requested are not available or, if available, are of dubious quality. For every request, home office should ask: Is this information necessary to help us manage the subsidiary or the broader worldwide operations? If so, is it worth the cost of collection? These questions are routinely asked before conducting marketing research; yet inside the company it is often assumed that management time is a free commodity. Similarly, information that is sent to the overseas subsidiary should pass the same test.

Subsidiary managers must likewise understand that the home office has information needs that they should strive to meet. The practice of keeping separate sets of books, one for home office and one for operations in Brazil, may bolster executive egos but it destroys the opportunity for the home office to assist or coordinate either Brazil or other operations.

Some companies manage intrafirm communications much better than others. This often requires a "need-to-know" justification for information requested from subsidiaries. An "information czar" might be located in the home office to filter requests before sending them to the subsidiary. This person might also expedite information needs of the subsidiary by directing them to appropriate positions in the company. This need for a home-office facilitator may be more acute for companies hiring nationals rather than expatriates as their subsidiary managers, since the nationals are less familiar with home-office procedures and politics.

The growing size and complexity of multinational operations will require an ever-greater flow of communications between home office and overseas affiliates. At the same time, for companies adopting a truly multinational posture there must be an associated loss of autonomy for subsidiary managers. For the continued success of such corporations, coordination and cooperation between home-office and subsidiary managers is essential. This coordination must avoid the rivalry, conflict, and antipathy that all too often characterize how subsidiary managers feel about their home office. While some tension exists in virtually all organizations, home-office managers might try to avoid exacerbating these feelings with arbitrary or excessive guidelines, restrictions, or pressures. The onus thus lies with home offices, as well as subsidiaries, to ensure that systems respond to changes in strategic posture. Without innovative ways to manage the information flow, managers may find themselves drowning in a sea of information designed to serve them. Without cooperative attitudes and relationships, changes in management systems are likely to result only in further waste and frustration.

REFERENCES

1. Characteristics that did not explain reporting differences included the level of worldwide and Brazilian sales, the number of foreign subsidiaries of the company, the type of industry, the volume and percentage of world sales outside the home-country market, the size of Brazilian sales compared with world sales, and the length of time established in Brazil.

2. Warren J. Keegan, "Multinational Scanning: A Study of the Information Utilized by Headquarters' Executives in Multinational Companies," *Administrative Science Quarterly* (September 1974), pp. 411-22.

3. It is interesting to note the results when home office managers of Japanese companies who were responsible for Brazilian operations were asked this question in reverse form. From their viewpoint in Japan, they recognized limitations in their understanding about Brazil, but they consistently claimed their understanding to be greater than it was perceived to be by their own subsidiary managers in Brazil.

4. William K. Brandt and James M. Hulbert, *The Multinational Corporation in Brazil: An Empirical Study* (Rio de Janeiro: Zaher Editores, 1976), Chap. 3.

5. Even though marketing was reported to afford the greatest freedom to subsidiary management, there are nevertheless a variety of marketing decisions that are generally not made at the subsidiary level.

6. J. Child, "Strategies of Control and Organizational Behavior," *Administrative Science Quarterly* (March 1973), p. 3.

7. Child, "Strategies of Control."

8. Brandt and Hulbert, *The Multinational Corporation in Brazil*, Chap. 5.

9. See Gordon Shillinglaw, "Divisional Performance Review: An Extension of Budgetary Control," in C. S. Bonini, R. J. Jaedicke, and H. M. Wagner, eds., *Management Controls: New Directions in Basic Research* (New York: McGraw-Hill Book Co., 1964), pp. 149-63.

9

MEETING THE CHALLENGE OF MULTINATIONAL MARKETING RESEARCH

by Lee Adler and Charles S. Mayer *

> . . . he laboured not only as a merchant, but also as a shipman
> . . . to Denmark and Flanders and Scotland; in all of which lands
> he found certain rare, and therefore more precious wares, which
> he carried to other parts wherein he *knew* them to be least
> familiar, and coveted by the inhabitants beyond the price of
> gold itself; wherefore, he exchanged these wares for others
> coveted by men of other lands. . . .
>
> —*Life of St. Godric*, by Reginald,
> a monk of Durham, c. 1170 A.D.
> [italics added] .

How St. Godric, a merchant who later became a hermit, "knew"
we are not told, since marketing research in the Middle Ages was
primitive at best. What we are concerned with in this paper[1] is how
today's marketing manager can "know." The problems of obtaining
comparable multinational marketing information are many. The
organizational requirements for implementing and communicating
such information in a multinational firm also present stumbling
blocks. The purpose of this paper is to identify those features of
multinational marketing research that require special attention for
their effective implementation, administration, and control.

AN OVERVIEW

First, a definition. In the most comprehensive sense, *international
research* means research conducted in any single country except the

---

* Lee Adler is Professor of Marketing at Fairleigh Dickinson University, Madison, New Jersey. Charles S. Mayer is Professor of Marketing at York University, Toronto, Canada.

marketer's home country. In a narrower sense, the term means multi-country research dedicated to solving a multicountry problem. It is this latter sense that we will adopt. The distinction is real and may have profound consequences for overseas research management. While many marketers talk of "international marketing," there may really be no such function for most firms. Rather, "international marketing" may be the sum of all local foreign programs, each tailored to the differences of unique markets with few ingredients in common.

The problems, goals, and methods of research overseas are no different from those at home. What differs is the detail. And the detail is all important because of cultural, social, economic, linguistic, psychological, and other variations from one nation to another.

To make this point clearer yet, let us consider the possible orientations of different marketers:

- A marketer whose product or service is truly international, for example, Trans World Airlines.
- A marketer whose product or service is provided in a given country, but who is substantially dependent on demand from other countries (e.g., Hertz Corporation, or world-famous hotels such as the Savoy in London or the Okura in Tokyo).
- A marketer whose product or service is bought by nationals of one or more countries, but is provided in other locations altogether (e.g., selling Caribbean cruises in Western Europe, or condominiums in The Gambia to Scandinavians).
- A marketer whose product or service may be sold in many countries, but is varied to suit local requirements or laws. In this instance, the orientation and, hence, information requirements will also depend on the amount of decentralized decision making at the local level (e.g., automobiles).
- A marketer whose product or service is sold in many countries, but is essentially unchanged across countries (e.g., Coca-Cola, Singer Sewing Machines, Schering Ethical Pharmaceuticals).

For each of these marketing types, the requirements for truly comparable multicountry data are different. If the marketer is concerned with a multicountry problem, then his research information for each country must be comparable to that of other countries. For example, the Hertz car rental system in each Western European nation is strongly dependent for its business on reservations made in other Western European countries. It is therefore incumbent on Hertz research to be so designed and managed as to permit comparable readings. Other international marketers may be able to operate quite successfully in a given country without comparability with other countries. Even in these situations, however, comparability may be extremely useful for two reasons:

- So that *priorities* may be determined
- So that marketing knowledge acquired in one country may be transferred, where practical, to other countries

It should be stressed that we do not mean compatibility in a narrow, technical sense. All too often, inexperienced researchers seek comparability by simultaneously trying to use the same sampling plan and questionnaire in a number of countries. This kind of mindless replication is doomed to failure because of linguistic, cultural, social, political, attitudinal, and other differences. *True* comparability, paradoxical as it may sound, is often achieved by varying research methods.

Unfortunately, the even greater demands made on researchers by multinational requirements are not supported by the state of the art. Generally speaking, the international portion of company research operations is less well developed than its domestic counterpart. Concurrently, with the notable exception of a handful of countries, it is more difficult to find able practitioners and research houses abroad.

To these factors we must add what appears to be an even lower level of understanding and appreciation of research on the part of international line executives than is true among their domestic peers. Likewise, in portraying the international climate, we must bear in mind a slower pace, impeded by mail strikes, revolutions, and lost telexes.

PROBLEMS IN INTERNATIONAL RESEARCH AND HOW TO SOLVE THEM

We have provided a foretaste of the unique problems confronting international researchers. These problems arise from:

- National differences
  - Language
  - Consumption patterns
  - Attitudes, traditions, mores
- Economic differences
- Cultural differences
- Market structure differences
- Differences in research facilities and conduct

All of these factors must be reckoned with in research design and implementation, and all have profound implications for our particular managerial orientation. To set the stage, let us examine some of these differences in more detail.

National Differences

As one example of the problems encountered, the 1963 *Reader's Digest* study of consumer behavior in a number of Western European countries astonished everyone by reporting that France and West Germany consumed more spaghetti and macaroni than Italy.[2] Proportions of households using these products in the home were:

France	90%
West Germany	71%
Italy	63%
Luxembourg	61%
Belgium	45%
Netherlands	45%

The reason for this curious finding was that the question posed dealt with packaged and branded spaghetti and macaroni—while many Italians buy their spaghetti loose. The *Reader's Digest* recognized this point in a footnote. Nevertheless, the question, as asked, did not provide—as it was intended to—a valid comparison among the six countries.

Economic Differences

Market segments vary so drastically on both inter- and intra-country bases as to require quite different sample designs even for studies needing multicountry comparability. For example, the market for many common packaged goods—foods, over-the-counter drugs, cosmetics, and the like—is limited to the upper social strata in many developing countries, in contrast to very broad usage in the developed lands. It would be wasteful to include in the sampling plan the whole population in all countries where these products are sold. Indeed, the sampling frame as well as the method of selection of respondents can be expected to vary significantly among countries.

Cultural Differences

Cultural differences may also occasion very sharp differences in research design. The examples of these differences are legion:

- In England, Germany, and Scandinavia, beer is generally perceived as an alcoholic beverage. By contrast, in the Mediterranean countries, beer is seen as more akin to a soft drink. Therefore, a study of beer in northern Europe that wished to examine its competitive status would have to build in questions on wines and distilled spirits. In Italy, Spain, and Greece, on the other hand, the comparison would have to be with soft drinks.
- Or, consider bar chocolate. In Italy, it is quite common for children to have a bar of chocolate between two slices of bread as a snack. In France, bar chocolate is often used in cooking. But a West German would be surprised by either of these uses.
- In Thailand, very few people have a hot drink before they leave for work, because charcoal is the normal cooking fuel and it takes a long time to heat. So Thais will stop at a street cafe on the way to work to have a hot drink. Obviously, a study on these beverages in Thailand would have to pose very different questions from those used in other countries.

Market Structure Differences

Competitive factors will obviously play a major role in research design. For example, suppose the topic under investigation is the sales potential of a new cleaning product in Holland, Belgium, and

151

Germany. The problem is the same in each country: to estimate consumer acceptability. Yet the research itself has to vary considerably if the level of competition (i.e., stage in product life cycle) is different. In Germany, for instance, there may already be a good many similar, well-entrenched products. The inquiry would have to determine if the market would absorb another brand and what competitive vulnerabilities to counterattack might exist. On the other hand, if there was no comparable product in Belgium, the study would need to concentrate on acceptance of the product concept and how it might compete against alternative ways housewives accomplish the same function. Between these extremes, if in Holland there were one or two rival brands, each newly launched, the mission of research would be to measure their penetration to date and the reasons for their apparent success or failure.

Other factors that may crucially affect research design and management include:

- Legal constraints
- Physical distribution facilities
- Tariff and other import regulations
- Conventions in selling policies and practices, pricing discounts, and service levels
- Geographic concentration (or scatter)
- Media configurations

Differences in Research Facilities and Conduct

In the United States, there is a trend toward greater use of the telephone for survey research. Yet this is scarcely possible in most other countries, even those considered advanced on other criteria, both because of the low incidence of telephone ownership and the quality of service.

Mail surveys are easily conducted in the United Kingdom and Germany, but high illiteracy rates in Italy and Spain would militate against successful mail studies in these latter countries. Moreover, the reliability of mail service would further confound the problem.

Cultural differences also interact with research methods. For instance, it is relatively easy to get groups of working-class German

152

women into a central location for focused group interviews. In Southern Italy or Spain, however, the recruiter would be regarded with great suspicion. The women would probably have to consult their husbands or the local priest first.

Long questionnaires do not seem to be much of a problem in the United States. But they are in Hong Kong, where everyone seems to rush breathlessly about. And they are a problem in Brazil, too, but for another reason. In Brazil, even short questionnaires have a way of becoming long, because Brazilians are very conscientious and literal-minded in trying to answer honestly and fully.

In some countries it is hard to interview men during the day. But they may be interviewed readily in the early evening or, surprisingly, in the early morning. In other countries, notably the Moslem and Asian lands, there may be some resistance to in-home interviewing, and so respondents must be plied with questions on the doorstep or in the street.

The raw material for drawing a probability sample varies considerably from country to country. In some countries, reliable electoral registers, local maps for selecting blocks and planning interviewers' routes, and comprehensive auto registration lists are available; while in others only incomplete and outdated lists can be found. The location of these lists is also a factor in research administration. In Great Britain, for example, a central electoral register is maintained in London for the entire country. By contrast, in Italy the voter lists are kept in each commune, of which there are over 9,000.

The above examples suggest why it is so difficult to obtain comparable data in multicountry research. Recognizing differences among countries is certainly important. However, responding to them in meaningful ways is the only way to obtain comparable results. While such responses clearly depend on technical competence for their implementation, such competence is not generally the scarce ingredient. What is lacking, and what we wish to draw attention to, is the administration of multinational research.

MULTINATIONAL RESEARCH ADMINISTRATION

From the experience of international researchers, it is possible to adduce a number of useful practices and to note some pitfalls to be avoided. Of these, perhaps the most important is the selection of the right research agency, and so we start with this topic.

Selecting Research Agencies

Assuming a multinational study is needed, one of the more controversial questions which of three possible kinds of agencies the research sponsor should choose:

- A multinational agency with owned-and-operated branches in several countries
- A network of independently owned local agencies operating as a chain and coordinated for a particular study by one member
- A group of independently owned local agencies assembled and coordinated by the study sponsor

To deal adequately with these possibilities, we need to return to the issue of comparability. To start, we must recognize the distinction between comparability at the data-collection stage and comparability at the interpretation stage. While comparability at the data-collection stage may be technically tidy, it may also defeat the objectives of the study. What is vital is to get comparable results. The questionnaire, the sample design and composition, and the methods used may all have to be different to obtain comparable results. In other words, comparability is concerned with ends, not means.

It follows, therefore, that the achievement of comparability of results calls for a high degree of centralized planning, control, and analysis of data. If the corporate research department is truly able to supply this caliber of coordination, then the field arrangements may be local only. On the other hand, if the company's international research capability is limited, as is true in most corporate circumstances, it behooves the firm to seek strong external support. This is likelier to come from a multinational agency. It is not essential for the central agency to own local agencies in each country involved. What is essential is the assumption of central responsibility.

The need to respect national differences and adapt research techniques to cope with them may appear to be in conflict with this

154

stress on central planning and control. But the conflict is more apparent than real. An able central agency will know where to turn and how to judge national factors so as to avoid cultural and social traps.

Research companies in different countries vary not only in quality, but also in the techniques they use. As in domestic research, marriage to a given technique is a hidden reef that may cause the stoutest of research ships to founder. Moreover, on occasion, the local "knowledge" may be a hindrance. It is sometimes better not to know all the things that cannot be done. For example, when Western firms first sought to arrange for lengthy personal interviews in Japan, the local research houses insisted that it would be very difficult to persuade respondents to spend long periods answering questions at the door— the predominant practice of the time. The obvious suggestion was to carry out the interviews inside the home. The Japanese demurred, noting that it would be contrary to good manners for interviewers to invite themselves into strangers' homes. Finally, an experiment was conducted in which one team of interviewers was asked to conduct one day's quota of interviews in-home. No problem was encountered. In fact, the interviewers were treated with great courtesy, offered tea and even offered saki and food.

How, then, does one go about selecting a research firm? Let us first assume that the researcher is trying to assemble a group of independent research agencies operating in several countries. Let us further assume that the researcher has *no* knowledge of each country's research facilities. The best starting point is to do some research at home first. Useful sources of information include the following:

1. Friends, associates, and professional colleagues experienced in multinational research. This is the best single source. Indeed, international researchers in noncompetitive industries often exchange information on foreign research agencies on an informal, continuing basis in order to keep up with strong and weak performers.
2. Directories of research agencies, such as the ones published by the American Marketing Association, the British Market Research Society, and the European Society for Opinion and Marketing Research. These lists offer no judgment on quality,

of course, nor are they complete. But they are a good jump-ing-off point.

3. Local associates, suppliers, and other sources, including:
   - The company's local managers.
   - Local advertising agencies. Note that some local advertising agencies may offer research services themselves, which may make them either potential suppliers of research or biased informants.
   - Government agencies.
   - Local telephone directories, many of which have Yellow Pages or the equivalent.

Having built an information base, there is no substitute for an on-site visit to each prospective agency. It will be found that agencies fall into several categories:

- Highly qualified, full-service agencies, either with or without an affiliation with an international network of agencies. They will vary in the kinds of research they are experienced in, such as consumer versus industrial, but no more so than at home.
- Agencies able to conduct fieldwork and data processing, but not strong enough to assist with research design, analysis, interpretation, and report writing. These will be recognized as the counterparts of domestic "field and tab" houses.
- Marketing, business, or economic consultants skillful in their own domains, but having only a general acquaintance with research. These firms are users of research rather than doers of research. One should be on guard against commissioning them to execute surveys if they represent themselves as being able to do so. They may learn at the sponsor's expense or may subcontract the study while providing inadequate super-vision.
- Hustlers, charlatans, and "thieves."

Since it is not always easy to distinguish between the wheat and the chaff, especially in developing nations, there are some practical guideposts to follow:

- If the research agency resists a visit to its office, offering instead to come to the prospective client's hotel or office,

156

beware. It is wise to inspect their facilities to see the nature of their capabilities.

- Prove for technical details. Inquiries about how a random sample would be drawn, for example, are very informative. Even more useful are inquiries about fieldwork: how interviewers are recruited, trained, and supervised; how experienced they are; how fieldwork is validated.
- Ask for their client list and check references.
- Examine copies of recent reports they have prepared in noncompetitive industries to determine how well they are able to organize material and their written skill in English—if a written report in English is called for.

If the researcher cannot visit the agencies himself, he has two sound alternatives to choose between:

- Select a large multinational agency or the standard bearer of a multinational chain of agencies and let their home office assume full responsibility for the local efforts.
- Retain an independent international research consultant or free-lancer. There are a small number of these people, who have usually served as international research executives with large firms before hanging out their own shingles. They will know the local research houses well or will know how to find out about them in short order.

The risk to avoid, however, is innocently sending the same questionnaire and fieldwork to a group of independent "reputable" local agencies, and then expecting a cohesive result. Either the corporate researcher must find the time, resources, and ability to select his research suppliers individually and to control the multicountry study himself, or he must seek this capability externally.

Handling Communications Problems

The substantive problems in dealing with language differences are of great consequence in multinational research. But here we will deal only with the facets of these problems that are within the scope of our managerial concerns. Useful practices include:

- If reducing research plans, proposals, contracts, and other documents to writing is vital at home, it is infinitely more important in foreign dealings. Lavish detail is to be recommended; it is almost impossible to be overabundant of detail.
- Many overseas research houses have someone on the staff who is fluent, or reasonably fluent, in English. But even "reasonable fluency" may be a trap. Indeed, it may be a worse trap than obvious deficiency in English because it may lull the English-speaking researcher into a false sense of security.

When dealing with researchers whose native tongue is not English, it is sound practice to engage in "back-translation" to expose semantic problems—that is, to have material translated from English into the other language. Then have a third party translate it back into English. Alfred Boote of Pepsico provides the example that when management wanted to use a successful Australian theme, "Baby, It's Cold Inside," in Hong Kong, by the time it was translated back into English from Cantonese it became "Small Mosquito, on the Inside It Is Very Cold."[3] Although small mosquito is the colloquial term for small child, the intended meaning had been lost through back-translation.

- If the overseas research firm has been engaged to write a final report, it should be written directly in English rather than translated into English. If one's judgment is that a foreign research firm cannot write a lucid report in English, the wisest alternative may be to receive tables only and write the report at home.

Maintaining Control

Many of the best practices in domestic research apply equally well abroad. But there are some special "wrinkles" worthy of attention:

- Americans' sense of time differs from that of many non-Americans. Many Americans experience time as a vessel to be filled, as an enemy to be killed, as a conspirator to be outwitted, or as a long-distance runner to pace. Most foreigners, mercifully for them, are more relaxed about time. It is, therefore, useful to agree on timetables in writing, to check

158

progress frequently against due dates, and to keep after foreign researchers as necessary.

- In scheduling studies, beware of calendar differences. In the Mideast, for example, at least five different calendars are used, all of which are considerably different from our Gregorian calendar. This caution is recommended in addition to allowing for seasonal and religious differences.

- Look into differences in research ethics. They vary considerably from country to country. In a number of European countries, ethics are at least as stringent as in the United States. For example, one important test-market project in Scandinavia on behalf of a client in the travel field was nearly aborted because, for an unanticipated reason, it became necessary for the client's headquarters research agency in London to have a list of the names of first-wave respondents to check against previous consumption of the service involved. The Copenhagen-based research house was so scrupulous about releasing respondents' names as to refuse to let its British affiliate have them: even though the names were drawn from the client's customer list to begin with, strong guarantees were given in writing that the client would not see the names and, in any event, the names were not connected with individual responses.

At the other extreme, some overseas researchers do not hesitate to work for competitive clients concurrently, or even to sell confidential data collected for one client to competitors. Obviously, precautions need to be taken to guard against such occurrences.

- If at all possible, it is wise to establish checkpoints at critical stages of a project and to review the work personally. Time permitting, some of these checks can be handled by mail and phone, such as questionnaire construction, sampling plan, and review of marginals to decide on analytical groups for the tabulation plan. Others merit a personal visit. For example, if the researcher can be present when the interviewers are briefed, he can directly answer the inevitable unanticipated question and perhaps prevent some horror from occurring.

It is also useful to review the first several days of fieldwork to be sure everything is going well. Even if the researcher responsible for a project is not conversant in the language, it

159

is worth examining questionnaires for completion and asking for rough oral translations from the local agency to ensure that the questions are working as intended.

Organizing for International Research

It should be clear from the foregoing that multinational research is sufficiently different from domestic research to require separate treatment. Assuming that the volume of work warrants it, we believe that company research departments should have a separate, well-qualified international unit, even if it is a "one-man band." Of course, if the volume of work does not justify a full-time practitioner, then one of the staff members will have to devote part of his time to multinational work. From the standpoint of building up a body of experience, it is wiser to have one man responsible for all international studies. If, however, the department is organized along product, divisional, or functional lines, then international projects might logically be assigned to each specialist. Yet another factor is that international studies are usually regarded as a "plum" if they involve overseas travel. They are sometimes used as a way of rewarding worthy staff members.

In both formal and informal interviews with large multinational corporations, we found that in general the international research component was less well developed than the domestic one, though policies and practices were the same. Thus:

- Divisions operating abroad are expected to supply their own knowledge of foreign markets. If a division has enough overseas volume, it is likely to have a researcher formally assigned to the international sector. Or it may turn partially or wholly to the headquarters research department for support. Since operating components are less likely to be well staffed on the international side than on the domestic front, they tend to turn more often to a corporate staff for overseas assistance than do domestic units.
- The central research department, if there is one, is likely to carry out studies mostly on behalf of the larger corporate interest. For example, a study might be undertaken to consider the pros and cons of entering a given foreign industry via an acquisition.

- Just as domestic researchers are to be found lodged "all over the place," so, too, are international researchers. They may be located in the profit centers, at group and/or corporate headquarters, in special units, attached to the staffs of key officers, and so on.
- Reporting relationships for international research units are in keeping with those of the parent research department. The divisional international research manager will report to the divisional research director, but if the research director has a formal or a "dotted-line" relationship with a corporate research officer, the divisional international researcher will have his own professional relationship with the corporate international research unit head. In some large diversified American concerns, the international researchers in the divisions have, in effect, a separate professional mutual-help "society" operating informally. In several firms, they even meet periodically to exchange data, insights, and helpful experiences.
- Research organization may sometimes reflect a desire to budget frugally while providing needed services. In one large multinational corporation, researchers are stationed in key cities—such as Geneva, Hong Kong, and Sao Paolo—and financed jointly by the operating divisions using them.
- The exception to these arrangements occurs in the case of international firms so large as to merit researchers responsible solely for certain regions. For example, there are a number of giant multinational corporations in the packaged foods, drugs, cosmetics, and toiletries industries that have research managers assigned to, say, Latin America, the Far East, and Europe, respectively.

The above are, of course, general tendencies. Even more so than in the domestic sector, there is no one right answer in international research. The firms surveyed revealed diverse, individual behavior mirroring their needs of the moment.

- One firm, which dismissed its domestic corporate research staff for economy reasons, retained all of its international researchers stationed abroad. Management reasoned that they had the expertise to buy research services as needed in the United States, but lacked that competence abroad.

161

- Another firm reassigned its international staff members from corporate headquarters into its operating units.
- Still a third firm is "beefing up" its international staff at the corporate level, this being the only place where they feel they can achieve "critical mass."

The above types of organization deal with international marketing as it affects the U.S.-based overseas activities of the particular company. Yet other modes exist where there are divisions, subsidiaries, joint-venture partners, or franchises, entirely located abroad. These entities, to the degree to which they operate autonomously, their problems insist, and their size permits, will have their own research departments. In these cases, contact with the central corporate office is likely to be inhibited by geographic separation, if not by political considerations and national mores.

There is a high probability that the number and caliber of research professionals in these overseas arms will be disappointing relative to headquarters' standards. The reasons for this are rooted in management's lack of appreciation of what research can do, stemming either from a lack of knowledge or from negative attitudes. Our "favorite" illustration is that of the Europe-based toiletries manufacturer who maintained a wholly owned subsidiary in the United States. The advertising agency of the U.S. subsidiary, finding that the company had literally no knowledge of its U.S. market, repeatedly proposed a basic consumer market study. The proposal went so far as to include a draft questionnaire because the client had so little knowledge of research practice. The head of the subsidiary recognized the need for the data but was not empowered to authorize the study without home-office approval. Accordingly, when the chief marketing executive paid his next visit to New York, the proposal was presented to him. After reading it, he said: "I don't see why you need to spend all this money. I travel around personally a lot in the states in our field. I will tell you the answers." He then proceeded to answer all the questions as if he were the entire sample; criticized the agency personnel, who were sitting there, jaws slack and eyes glazed, for not recording his responses; and rejected the proposal.

This kind of scenario is more likely to occur when experienced researchers from the home office visit countries other than the more sophisticated ones. It is *the* basic obstacle multinational researchers must overcome in order to make further advances.

162

CONCLUSION

As the commercial world continues to shrink, and as national boundaries cease to be meaningful in terms of trade, corporations will have to broaden their marketing horizons. In doing so, they will encounter the need for better, more comparable, and more actionable multicountry data.

Multinational research presents some unique problems. Perhaps the most important is the requirement of comparability despite differences in language, consumption patterns, attitudes, economic development, culture, market structure, and available research facilities. And by comparability we mean comparable results, not mindless replication of technique!

While the problems of multinational research are solved through the skillful adaptation of research techniques to each environment, such adaptation is more likely to depend on the administrative and organizational ability of the supervising researcher than on his technical competence.

One such administrative task is the selection, supervision, and control of possibly several research agencies involved in the multicountry research. We explored potential alternatives. Next we turned our attention to insuring that adequate communications exist between local researchers and the central coordinator. We also suggested areas for special concern in controlling the multicountry study.

Multinational research is sufficiently different from domestic research to warrant a separate organizational structure. On the basis of interviews with large multinational firms, we identified different approaches to organizing for multinational research. While there is no one right answer, we believe that this is an area that deserves careful managerial attention. It is through the appropriate organizational relationships and managerial responsibilities that the multinational firm can insure the development of meaningful and managerially actionable multinational marketing research.

The basic deterrent to more meaningful multinational research lies rooted in the understanding and appreciation of international line

163

executives for such data. To overcome this obstacle, researchers must prove the value of their results to managers. Such proof is far more likely to depend on the researchers' managerial competence than on their facility with research technique.

REFERENCES

1. This paper is based on a chapter of the authors' forthcoming book, *Marketing Research: A Managerial Approach*. It in turn draws heavily on three papers presented at the 1975 International Conference of the American Marketing Association, held in Chicago. Rather than having each page bristle with *"op. cit.'s"* and *"ibid.'s"* we credit the three sources here:

    Lee Adler, "Managing Marketing Research in the Diversified Multinational Corporation"; in Edward M. Mazze. ed;. *1975 Combined Proceedings*. Chicago: American Marketing Assn., 1975.

    Morten M. Lenrow, "Why Are You Afraid to do International Marketing Research—When You're Already Halfway Home?"; in Edward M. Mazze, ed., *1975 Combined Proceedings*. Chicago: American Marketing Assn., 1975.

    Paul Howard Berent, "International Research is Different"; in Edward M. Mazze, ed., *1975 Combined Proceedings*. Chicago: American Marketing Assn., 1975.

2. European Market Survey, *Readers' Digest Association*, 1963.

3. A. S. Boote, "Cultural Myopia," talk delivered to the International Marketing Group, American Marketing Assn., New York, May 1, 1969; as reported in Robert Ferber, ed., *Handbook of Marketing Research* (New York: McGraw-Hill Book Co., 1974).

10

RESEARCH FOR MULTINATIONAL PRODUCT POLICY

by Yoram Wind *

INTRODUCTION

Product policy is the cornerstone of the multinational marketing mix. The products or services a company chooses to sell to the selected target market constitute the basis for development of the company's world-wide marketing program and determine the company's role in the world market, in relation to both customers and competitors. Decisions with regard to the nature, depth and breadth of the product line sold throughout the world and the importance attached to new product development influences the global image of the company as well as its rate of growth and success in world markets. Product policy decisions reflect the company's positioning and segmentation strategies and hence are closely related to promotional, distribution and pricing decisions.

In planning the international product decisions, the international marketing manager has to determine the number, range and type of products to be sold throughout the world, and what new products should be developed for which markets and countries; what products should be added, modified, and deleted from the overall product line in each national market and when, what brand names should be used, how products should be packaged and what post sales services should be provided in each of the markets in which the company operates throughout the world. Clearly, a formidable task!

In making these decisions, a considerable amount of information is required. This stems not only from the need to deal with more

---

*Yoram Wind is Professor of Marketing, The Wharton School, University of Pennsylvania.

than a single country and consider the effect of additional sets of environmental factors (cultural, legal, economic, technological and other characteristics of the target countries), but also from management lack of familarity with the foreign markets.

Yet, despite this need for more and better multinational marketing information as inputs to multinational product decisions, and the growing (current and potential) share of corporate profits generated from multinational operations, multinational product research has received relatively little attention. This is evident, for example, if one examines the size of multinational product research budgets in consumer and industrial firms which are considerably smaller than their domestic counterparts.

Given the high cost of multinational research the smaller size of the multinational product research budgets may be justified, if the type of research required as input to multinational product decisions is somewhat different than the research process followed domestically. One may argue, for example, that in many situations one should not engage in costly new product introductory consumer research in foreign countries, and that a suitable alternative might be obtaining the services of a local importer who would try to sell the product and provide the exporter "free" marketing information on consumers' response (purchases) of the product. Similarly, a local advertising agency might serve as an "expert informer" on the characteristics of the given market. Whereas such alternatives might be acceptable under certain conditions (e.g., firms with limited resources and commitment to international operations), it can lead to lost opportunities and has its associated costs and risks.

The determination of the desired type of multinational product research requires a better understanding of the multinational product policy decisions and the problems associated with multinational marketing research.

Multinational product (and marketing) studies, should be based on the same *approach* utilized in domestic marketing research studies. It should be composed of a systematic problem definition and model

166

building leading to a research design, data gathering, and data analysis and interpretation for the purpose of improved marketing strategy.

In designing and carrying out product related studies in other countries, researchers often follow the conceptual and methodological procedures common in the United States. Yet, management research needs and resources, the available marketing research services and data, and the environmental conditions (including the research infrastructure) vary widely across countries requiring the consideration of country (or group of countries) idiosyncratic research approaches. It is desirable, therefore, to design product (and marketing research) programs for each country (or group of countries) separately, focusing, however, on required commonality across countries to enable compatability of results, achieve economics of scale and employ the same research design in multicountry studies. Hence, the decision to utilize the same research approach and instrument in several countries should be based on an explicit examination of the idiosyncratic research related characteristics of the various countries.

No single approach can, therefore, be designed as guidelines for product related research around the world. The design and implementation of research activities for multinational product policy should be based on a clear understanding of: (a) the unique characteristics involved in conducting research in other countries (such as the diversity, across countries, in availability and quality of data, data collection methods, personal and research hardware as well as the language and cultural difficulties involved in conducting cross cultural studies)[1]; and (b) the nature of the product decisions involved and the type of information inputs they require.

Since both of these topics can benefit from an interaction among multinational product managers and researchers and interested academicians, the objective of this paper is to provide the initial

---

[1] It is outside the scope of this paper to discuss the unique characteristics of multinational marketing (and other social) research. The interested reader may review the following sources: Lee 1966, Wind and Robinson 1970, Mitchell 1965, Sears 1961, Sechrest, Fay and Zadia 1972, Triandis 1972, Andersen 1967 and Webster 1960.

input for such a dialogue by focusing on the key multinational product decisions and their associated information (and research) needs.

The discussion on multinational product policy is divided into three major sections: Planning the International Product Mix, Product Design and Modification and Product Deletion.

PLANNING THE INTERNATIONAL PRODUCT MIX[2]

The first step in planning the product mix is to establish overall policy guidelines. This includes determining the number and range of products to be developed, manufactured and marketed in various countries, the emphasis to be placed on new product development and innovativeness in world markets, the interdependencies between product decisions and the country selection and entry decision, and the allocation of corporate resources among products and markets.

While the same basic factors have to be taken into consideration in developing the international or domestic product mixes, their nature and impact may differ requiring management to have information on:

- *Customer Interests and Characteristics*: As in domestic marketing, the examination of customer characteristics in selected markets provides the basis for determining the feasible set of products and most appropriate product line. However, how important are new models, different packaging, product improvement, or the specific product benefits to customers in various countries? Similarly, what assortment of products are desired and purchased in various countries?
- *Competitive Marketing Offerings*: What is the type and range of products offered by competitors in the various countries?

---

[2]The material in this section is partially based on the product policy chapter in Y. Wind and S. P. Douglas, *International Marketing Management* (Forthcoming) and the Multinational Product Policy chapter in Y. Wind *Product Policy* (Forthcoming).

Has the demand for a given type of product been already met by competition? What is the range of products and marketing policies of competitors and should they be matched?

- *Company Objectives and Resources*: What are the firms' objectives in overseas expansion—growth, market share, reduction of risks, exporting declining local products, etc.? Does the product line make optimal use of company resources and competitive advantages relative to overseas markets, such as, for example, superior technology or management and marketing skills?

- *Objectives and Policies of Intermediate Marketing Organizations*: While management might prefer to concentrate on a limited number of high turnover items, distributors' preferences may necessitate offering a full product line. Information on the type, number, character and preference of intermediate marketing organizations is thus essential.

- *Other Environmental Factors*: A variety of other environmental factors may affect the product mix strategies; legal restrictions on the range and type of products which may be sold, or the combinations of products which may be sold by a given type of retail outlet; regulations on product content or packaging, differential tariff barriers or taxation on different items in a product line, etc.

- *Mode of Entry*: The selected mode of entry is also a key factor both influencing and resulting from product mix decisions. Use of export channels may enable concentration on a limited number of the more profitable items; if overseas sales are limited, this may in fact be the only solution. The establishment of production facilities in various foreign markets may have similar effect of providing relatively limited number of products. Alternatively, establishment of an overseas sales subsidiary may necessitate offering a full line of products. Furthermore, different modes of entry are associated with varying degrees of product diversity among markets.

The diversity of these six factors, both within and among countries, suggest that the international product mix of a company may range from a simple one product exported to one or a few countries to an extremely complex mix of numerous product lines which vary across countries. The former case is quite typical of small

169

firms whose exporting activities are only incidental to their domestic operations. This mode of operation, although quite reasonable for this stage of the firm's international operations, may be the beginning of a process of "creeping commitment" for international operations which may result in a nonoptimal international product mix which often results from having varied product lines in different countries. Management has, therefore, to follow a more explicit and rigorous approach to the determination of the most desirable product mix. The approach suggested to achieve an optimal international product mix (both within and across countries) is the *product portfolio approach* (Wind, 1974). This approach is a somewhat modified application of portfolio theory to the product mix decision. The major assumptions of this approach are:

1) The two most relevant characteristics of a product portfolio are its expected return and its riskiness (which reflect the market's conditional response functions);
2) Managers will choose to hold efficient portfolios which are those which
   (a) maximize expected returns for a given degree of risk, or alternatively and equivalently,
   (b) minimize risk for a given expected return.

The notion of an efficient portfolio can be seen in the following hypothetical example:

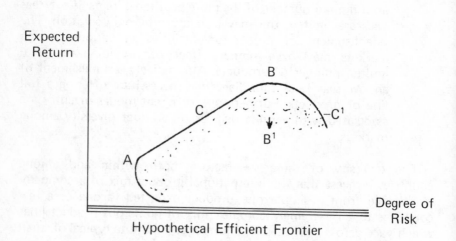

Hypothetical Efficient Frontier

Assume that the shaded area represents all possible product portfolios that can be obtained from a given set of products. Portfolios lying on the curve AB are efficient since they offer the maximum return for any given level of risk and minimum risk for any given level of return. Any portfolio to the right of point B, such as C^1, is on the boundary of the feasible set, but is not efficient, since portfolio C on the curve AB offers the same expected return at a lower risk. Similarly, any portfolio on the efficiency curve is superior to any portfolio in the shaded area. For example, portfolio B offers, at the same level of risk as B^1, a considerably higher expected return.

3) It is theoretically and operationally possible to identify efficient portfolios by a systematic analysis of information for each of n products. The information is:
   (a) expected return estimates for all n products in k markets.
   (b) expected variation of the rate of return for all n products in k markets; and
   (c) all the expected covariances between the n products by the markets rates of return.

   These statistical inputs can be generated by a number of approaches ranging from projections of *ex post* data, through econometric procedures to *ex ante* estimates of probability distribution.

The analytical procedures used in portfolio analysis can range from simple graphs to the use of calculus or quadratic programming. The output could provide a suggested proportion of the total product mix which should be allocated to each product and market in order to achieve efficiency (i.e., maximization of return for a given degree of risk, including political risks, or the minimization of risk for a given expected return), given management's preference for a tradeoff between expected return and risk (assessed, for example, via conjoint scaling—Green and Wind, 1975).

Conceptually, the firm's multinational product portfolio can be extended to cover not only various products but combinations of products/markets. The difficulties in implementing the product portfolio suggest, however, that its major immediate value is in suggesting a framework for evaluating alternative product/market

171

mixes on their expected return and risk characteristics. In this context, management has to determine the amount of effort to be devoted to finding and developing new markets and the importance attached to developing new products. Johnson (1957) suggests that all product strategies can be classified along these two dimensions of product vs. market development.

In the international context, emphasis on *market development* implies that management pays primary attention to finding new uses, new customers and new markets throughout the world for the existing range of products sold by the firm. Management, therefore, attempts to capitalize on existing investment in product development and plant and tries to spread these over a larger volume of sales. Major effort is thus devoted to prospecting for new markets in other countries and to developing communication and distribution strategies to generate new customers, new uses, or make the product available in new areas.

The use of this type of strategy implies what Keegan (1969) has termed "a product extension" philosophy as management focuses on extending the market base for its products. Differences in the range of products available in different countries as well as barriers to the diffusion of ideas and information between countries makes this approach particularly appealing in international markets. The international company can thus take advantage of these differences and introduce an established or declining domestic product into another country as a "new" product, thus reaping the advantages of innovation without the cost of new product development.

A market development approach requires little marketing research effort and appears appropriate for firms with limited international objectives. Following this approach tends to lead to the use of overseas sales as a means of disposing of surplus domestic product. It may also be appropriate for small firms selling to a highly specialized target market. Here the most suitable approach is to extend the customer base by finding foreign market segments which exhibit similar characteristics to the firm's current domestic customers, rather than to try to reach *new* market segments in the home or foreign market. In any of these cases, reliance on export channels and little contact with the international markets can lead to lost opportunities by overlooking possible new uses for existing or modified products in overseas markets.

Emphasis on *product development* suggests that rather than focusing on expanding usage and finding new markets throughout the world for the existing line of products, management concentrates its attention on modifying existing products or developing new products for overseas markets. Thus management modifies or develops products geared to the specific needs and interests of overseas markets.

Quite often overseas market conditions require some product modifications. Differences in customer purchasing or usage patterns may suggest the desirability of adapting products in order to facilitate market penetration. For example, soap and detergents may be modified to meet local water conditions, household appliances modified to different usage conditions, soft drinks and food to taste preferences, and the like.

Alternatively, management may pursue an active policy of developing new products for existing or new overseas markets. This strategy is likely to be appropriate for companies with a high level of commitment to or involvement in overseas operations. It is typically a high risk strategy and requires a considerable amount of marketing research activities in the foreign markets. It may thus entail significant costs of product (technical) and marketing research and development.

While market development and product development are by no means mutually exclusive strategies, they are nonetheless important dimensions to be considered in developing international product policies. Concentration on market development implies that the main focus of the company's effort is likely to be centered on finding new markets overseas, exploring new opportunities, thus expanding the geographic scope of operations with respect to the company's current products. A focus on product development suggests that the company concentrates its attention on developing modified and new products for its existing domestic and international markets. While companies may pursue both directions simultaneously, such a strategy entails a major commitment of resources.

In all these cases, however, the marketing manager has to decide:

1) The desired level of international involvement;
2) The most appropriate strategies and allocation of resources among products and markets, given the expected return and risks of the various product/market strategies;
3) The desired target segments and product positionings for all the selected product/market strategies;
4) The most commensurate and efficient pricing, promotion and distribution strategies.

PRODUCT DESIGN AND MODIFICATION

The design of new products or the modification of existing products for overseas markets is at least as crucial an aspect of international product policy as it is in domestic marketing. One of the key issues in this context is whether to design and adapt products to different usage and environmental conditions in each overseas market, or whether to pursue a standardized (universal or regional) product policy. Two types of situations may be considered: Necessary and optional modifications.

Necessary product modifications involve, for example, electrical products which have to be adapted to different voltage systems, cars which have to be adapted for a left or right-hand drive, machinery to work under different climatic conditions, and other products to different weights or measurement systems. These types of adjustments are necessitated by differences in environmental factors such as measurement and calibration systems, language, product standards, and patent requirements.

In addition to these necessary changes there are other optional product modifications such as size, complexity, quality, style, design, and color which make the product more acceptable to the conditions of the target country.

While adaptation or modification to different market conditions and especially idiosyncratic cultural or language requirements may be appropriate under certain circumstances, it is not inevitably desirable. Much may depend on consumers anticipated reactions to the unchanged product and the size and composition of this segment. Certain products may carry prestige by virtue of the fact that they are not adapted to local market conditions, and hence some effort or cost is required to maintain or use them. The modification of products to each national environmental setting entails substantial cost and eliminates the possibility of spreading investment overheads and set-up costs over different markets. Cost considerations may suggest the appropriateness of product standardization rather than adaptation. Finally, the compatibility of product changes to management objectives, should be considered.

In making these and other product decisions, management has to consider not only the current market conditions but the expected future needs. While significant differences may exist between domestic and overseas markets at a given point in time, overseas markets may be developing in the same direction as the domestic market. For example, quality or price distinctions may be eliminated as similar target segments emerge in different countries. Hence, emphasis on national differences may not be the most desirable strategy in the long run.

All of these considerations require a considerable amount of product/marketing research input on current and future demand (and supply) trends, management's current and future objectives and resources, and relevant environmental trends.

The adaptation-standardization policy assumes in its most common form the existence of an established product. The guidelines provided by a standardization or adaptation policy is not limited, however, to existing products and is as relevant to the multinational firm's new product development decisions. The importance of the introduction of successful new products and services to the survival and growth of international firms requires, however, a more explicit consideration of the new product development system.

In determining the firm's multinational new product strategy a major decision should be whether the new products are to be developed by the firm (in the home country or elsewhere in the world) or alternatively acquired via mergers, acquisitions or product purchases.

In this latter case marketing as well as financial considerations are of prime importance requiring considerable input on product/marketing conditions and trends.

The objectives of an internal new product development system are to enable the firm to achieve its objectives with respect to new products in the most efficient manner. Such a system provides operational guidelines for (a) the key research stages required, and (b) the most appropriate organizational arrangements.

The philosophy underlying a "good" new product development system can be stated in terms of the following requirements to provide:

1) Top management commitment to the development and introduction of new products on a world-wide basis;
2) An opportunity for continuous management interaction and evaluation at each phase of the system;
3) A continuous and flexible system with multiple entry and termination points as well as the option of recycling and adapting to changing conditions;
4) A "fit" with the unique characteristics of the company (e.g., management style, objectives and resources) as well as an operational link between marketing, R&D and production;
5) A planned approach to new product development and introduction rather than involvement with new products as a result of a "creeping commitment";
6) Provisions for generation, development and evaluation of new products for specific market segments rather than for a total heterogeneous market (to utilize the "marketing concept");
7) Utilization of all the relevant tools—marketing research, management sciences, consumer behavior and the behavioral sciences.

Given these philosophical requirements, it is suggested that the international new product development system (very much like its domestic counterpart) follow seven major phases. These phases, their research needs and interrelationships are:

- *Setting Objectives*: The objectives for new product development should reflect the corporate overall objectives and

176

resources, management decisions concerning the desired level of international involvement, adaptability vs. modification strategy and the acceptable levels of risk and expected returns.

This agreed upon explicit set of objectives provides criteria for evaluation of any new product idea, as well as defining the boundaries for new product development. The objectives can be determined using unstructured brainstorming procedures or more rigorous structured procedures for the quantification of the various objectives according to their relative importance to the key international decision makers at both headquarters and relevant foreign operations.

- *Generation of Ideas*: The objectives of this phase is to generate a large number of new and innovative product ideas. A variety of research procedures have been utilized by various companies to generate new product ideas. These procedures involve quite frequently both consumers and "experts" utilizing a variety of structured and unstructured procedures. Among the more common consumer research procedures are focused group interviews and Kelly repertory grid as unstructured procedures and problem/benefit surveys, market structure and gap analysis as structured procedures. When using experts as respondents, brainstorming and the somewhat more structured Synectics approach have often been used as well as structured systematic procedures such as analogies, and the analysis of secondary sources.

In generating new product ideas, the participation of local operating units is quite essential since they are in close contact with the market and can provide an important source of information concerning customer problems and market trends, which may stimulate ideas for new products. In large multinational firms, international new product research units or committees may be formed as clearing houses for such ideas. Alternatively, in the case of an export operation, such information may be collected from the overseas sales force or import agent.

- *Idea/Concept Screening*: The screening and initial evaluation of new product ideas or concepts should be conducted with respect to:
  1) *Product and company characteristics*, such as compatibility with existing product line or channels of distribu-

tion, technical feasibility, compatibility with corporate objectives, and patentability.

2) *Market characteristics*, such as consumers' reactions to the concepts, and anticipated sales and growth potential.

The screening process involves two steps—corporate screening for compatibility and technical feasibility and market screening to assess consumers' reactions to the new concepts, and their perceived positioning by relevant market segments. The first of these procedures—the technical/managerial screening—(and the economic analysis which should be conducted at each stage of the new product development process) can be conducted either centrally or by the foreign units depending on the overall structure of the company's international operations. A meaningful consumer screening requires, however, some feedback from local organizational units which will conduct actual concept screening/testing procedures. For a discussion of such a procedure see Wind, 1973.

- *Product Development*: Responsibility for product development rests primarily with the R&D group which may be aided, however, by appropriate consumer studies (e.g., Green and Wind, 1975). The actual product development process can be centrally located or decentralized among various countries depending on the size and organizational structure of the firm as well as the nature and magnitude of the R&D activities, the relative importance of coordinating research and development ideas, and the degree of desired adaptation to each national market. Where the product has an important technological component and is uniform throughout the world, centralization is more appropriate. Where development activities focus predominantly on adaptation of existing products to local market conditions, for example, food products, decentralization may be preferred. In either case, to the extent that consumers or other market studies are desired as inputs to product design and formulation, packaging branding, and service offerings, it is essential to conduct the studies in the target markets.

A relatively ignored aspect of product research is the research for foreign buying. Selecting appropriate raw materials, products and services and identifying acceptable suppliers in the multinational arena is an extremely impor-

178

tant aspect of research, especially in periods of shortages. One of the major contributions of multinational product research can be in this area of foreign buying.

- *Concept/Product Evaluation*: The final stages in the product evaluation procedure may involve a second round of concept testing procedures, or more frequently an in-home use test with or without an accompanying test market. The primary objective of concept testing is to estimate the trial of the new product. In-home use tests, simulated test markets and test markets are primarily used to estimate repeat purchase probabilities. The evaluative procedures at this stage should provide specific diagnostic inputs for any necessary changes in product design, positioning or marketing strategy. A key question in undertaking this evaluative stage is whether management wants to test the product in each country separately, prior to launching in that country, or whether a single country is used as a test market area prior to world launching. This decision in turn depends to a large extent on whether modifications are made to meet different environmental conditions, whether substantially different response is anticipated in different countries, and whether the anticipated potential demand in a given national market is large enough to justify the costs involved in test marketing.

The minimum requirement of this stage of evaluation is to test locally the reaction of consumers, trade and other relevant organizations (e.g. government), to the product features, product positioning and its overall marketing strategy. Whether or not to conduct a test market depends on management familiarity and experience with the given market, the alternative strategies considered and obviously the costs involved.

In-home use test, mini test markets, and other substitute test market procedures are considerably cheaper than test markets and based on the United States experience are quite useful in estimating market share for alternative marketing strategies. In many multinational cases, however, test market is quite indispensible. It serves as a pilot operation to locate unanticipated problems and provide training and the necessary experience to the operating units. As such, test markets in the local foreign market are much more crucial than in the domestic markets. In entering such a test market, manage-

179

ment should have, however, well formulated strategies and should be ready to consider alternatives, such as withdrawing the new product, repositioning or modifying it, or proceeding toward full commercialization.

- *Development of a Marketing Strategy*: The objective of this phase is to develop the marketing strategy that is going to accompany the product introduction. The marketing plan should be developed prior to the test market stage and modified if necessary based on the results of test market.
- *Continuous Evaluation of Product Performance*: The objective of this phase is to develop a monitoring system to permit continuous evaluation of product performance providing guidelines for product repositioning and modification, changes in the marketing strategy, or product deletion. The development of an effective multinational monitoring procedure should involve the collection and analysis of both objective data on sales market share and profitability as well as subjective data on consumers reactions to the product, and its positioning. (Wind & Claycamp, 1976) As such, the design and implementation of a multinational monitoring system is not a trivial task. It requires the involvement of the local units, and the expert advice and commitment of headquarters.

PRODUCT ELIMINATION

The third decision area concerns the deletion and phasing out of weak products. In international as in domestic markets, primary attention is frequently given to the problem of developing, adding and modifying new products and less emphasis is placed on product deletion decisions. These are, however, no less critical, since keeping weak products can add substantially to overhead costs as well as diverting company resources from more profitable lines.

In international marketing, the deletion of products may be particularly critical in view of the scope of the problem and the rapidity of change in many international markets. Often the breadth and depth of the world-wide product line is greater than in the domestic market. It is thus important to ensure that weak products (based on estimated *future* profits and contribution to the product line) are phased out to prevent dispersion and fragmentation of effort. Furthermore, the rapid rate of change in international market conditions suggests the importance of continually monitoring products to examine their relevancy and contribution in the light of changing customer needs, competitive offerings and environmental (e.g., technological, legal, cultural, economic) conditions.

Appropriate organizational procedures for systematic review of products have, therefore, to be established. The criteria to evaluate product performance such as minimum level of sales, market share, profitability and contribution to the product line have to be determined. These can be established by local organizational units relative to specific market conditions, by headquarters' management, or by both, depending on the organizational structure. Some coordination of these criteria is typically desirable. The review of products based on these criteria may be carried out on a market by market and/or on a regional or global basis depending on the uniformity of the product mix in different markets. Typically, however, some information input from local organizational units is always necessary.

Decisions as to when to phase out products from national or regional markets and when to drop them altogether from the company's line should also be made. This again poses a number of issues concerning the uniformity of the world-wide product line. One approach is to phase out products in potentially weak markets while retaining them in markets where they are still profitable. Alternatively, one could consider the withdrawal of the product from all markets. The appropriate approach depends on opportunity and other costs associated with carrying the product in a limited number of countries and the autonomy of product management decisions. In any event, research should play a major role in providing the necessary inputs for these decisions.

CONCLUSION

In designing the firm's multinational product policy, management requires a considerable amount of continuous information about the market and about competitive and environmental conditions in other countries. This paper provides a brief review of the major multinational product decisions and some of their associated research needs. The issues involved in research for multinational product decisions were only occasionally touched upon. It might be useful, therefore, to conclude our discussion by identifying some of the key issues involved in research for multinational products. There are no clear cut answers to these issues and most of them are interrelated. It is hoped, however, that explicit attention to these and similar issues will stimulate further work in this area leading toward better understanding of multinational product research. Some of these issues are:

- How to overcome the limited availability and high cost of multinational marketing research?
- Can product research, in the form commonly used in the United States, be substituted for by the use of subjective evaluations of "local experts" or sequential market entry? What other alternatives can be utilized? Which specific research steps will they replace?
- How much should a company spend on multinational product research and how should the budget be allocated among the various product marketing strategies, products and markets? How can the theoretical concept of "cost and value" of information be utilized? What conditions determine the size and allocation of the budget?
- What is the most effective organizational structure—decentralized vs. centralized—of product/marketing management and marketing research?
- Should marketing research be done internally by the firm (marketing researchers as "doers") or outside (marketing researchers as brokers)?
- What should be the distribution of product/marketing research activities among various countries? Given that multinational companies operate in many countries, how should marketing research activities be allocated among the various countries?
- What is the effect of the firm's degree of commitment to and involvement in international operations on the nature and organization of multinational product research? What are the differences in the research activities of ethnocentric, polycentric, regiocentric or geocentric firms? (For a discussion of the differences among these orientations and their marketing implications see Perlmutter 1972, and Wind, Douglas and Perlmutter 1973].

- How can management deal effectively with the large hetero-
geneity of multinational markets?

One of the major obstacles for the effective use of multinational
product research is management attitude toward research. In contrast
to the belief in the research ethic prevalent in United States management circles, appreciation and use of research by management in
other countries is considerably less widespread. Management philoso-
phies and practice have traditionally emphasized the value of
experience and "wisdom" in decision-making, rather than vitality or
new original approaches (Noworthy, 1964). Confronted with this
attitude in most foreign countries the question is how can one
introduce local management to the research orientation and approaches, and how can one combine current management practices
with the newer research orientations?

REFERENCES

B. Andersen, "On the Comparability of Meaningful Stimuli in
Cross-cultural Research," *Sociometry*, Vol. 30 (June 1967), pp.
124-136.

P. E. Green and Y. Wind, "New Way to Measure Consumers'
Judgment," *Harvard Business Review,* Vol. 53 (July-August 1975),
pp. 107-117.

W. Keegan, "Multinational Product Planning: Strategic Alternatives," *Journal of Marketing*, Vol. 33 (January 1969), pp. 58-62.

S. C. Johnson, "How to Organize for New Products," *Harvard
Business Review*, Vol. 35 (May-June 1957), pp. 49-62; Vol. 33
(January 1969), pp. 58-62.

J. E. Lee, "Cultural Analysis in Overseas Operations," *Harvard
Business Review*, Vol. 44 (March-April 1966), pp. 106-114.

R. E. Mitchell, "Survey Materials Collected in Developing
Countries: Sampling Measurement and Interviewing Obstacles to
Intra- and Inter-National Comparisons," *International Social Science
Journal*, Vol. XVII (1965), pp. 665-685.

O. M. Noworthy, "American in European Management Philosophy," *Harvard Business Review*, Vol. 42 (March-April 1964), pp. 101-108.

H. V. Perlmutter, "The Multinational Firm and the Future," *Annals of the American Academy of Political and Social Science*, Vol. 403 (September 1972), pp. 139-152.

R. M. Sears, "Transcultural Variables and Conceptual Equivalence," in Bert Kaplan, *Studying Personality Cross-culturally* (Evanston, Illinois: Row Peterson and Co. 1961), pp. 445-455.

L. Sechrest, T. Fay and S. M. Zadia, "Problems of Translation in Cross-cultural Research," *Journal of Cross-cultural Psychology*, Vol. 3 (March 1972), pp. 41-56.

H. Triandis, *The Analysis of Subjective Culture* (New York: Wiley, 1972).

L. Webster, "Comparability in Multicountry Surveys," *Journal of Marketing Research*, Vol. 1 (November 1960), pp. 39-42.

Y. Wind, "A New Procedure for Concept Evaluation," *Journal of Marketing*, Vol. 37 (October 1973), pp. 2-11.

Y. Wind, "Product Portfolio: A New Approach to the Product Mix Decision," in R. C. Curham *Proceedings of the 1974 AMA conference*, pp. 460-464.

Y. Wind and H. J. Claycamp, "Planning Product Line Strategy: A Matrix Approach," *Journal of Marketing*, Vol. 40 (January 1976), pp. 2-9.

Y. Wind, S. Douglas and H. Perlmutter, "Guidelines for Developing International Marketing Strategy," *Journal of Marketing*, Vol. 37 (April 1973), pp. 14-23.

Y. Wind and P. J. Robinson, "Perceptual and Preference Mapping of Countries: An Application of Multidimensional Scaling," paper presented at the annual meeting of the Association for education in International Business, December 1970.